DIZZYING DEPTHS

LANCE MANION

ALSO BY LANCE MANION

Merciful Flush

Results May Vary

The Ball Washer

Homo sayswhaticus

The Trembling Fist

The Song Between Her Legs

What You Don't Understand

neXt

Tales of Adventure With Nap Lapkin

People ask me why I only write short stories.
It's a long story.

-Lance Manion

Forward: Note from the Editor

This is my ninth go at editing a collection of Manion stories. How did I get here? That's easy to answer: he made me laugh.

I downloaded *Ball Washer* several years ago and found myself actually laughing out loud - which, despite the ubiquitous text acronym LOL, is pretty rare. Life is hard; laughter is a gift. On a whim, I sent the author a message of appreciation and somehow, here we are.

On the face of it, we're very different. He's an Atheist; I'm a Christian. He's a misogynist; I'm a Bohemian. He's a Mondrian portrait; I'm a Picasso still-life. But we're both writers. Our primary modes of exploration are through ideas and words. In truth, misogyny and bohemianism are mere cloaks we wear and are easily set aside.

Manion knows his writing is not for the masses. He's turned down opportunities to dial down offensive content to be published on a larger scale. That's partly why I'm a fan. I may not agree with or even like some of his stories, but I firmly believe in free speech and not in the politically correct hole we find our culture drowning in.

That's not to say his manuscripts aren't a mess- they are. I'm just hoping I polish them enough so you can read his wit and not notice his utter lack of understanding of punctuation rules.

Manion has stated he believes a goal of creating is to be a catalyst for others. That is true in my case; though my attempts at storytelling have been awful, I've been encouraged to find my voice, which I have as a poet. Which he supports but mocks incessantly.

I hope you enjoy this book and maybe find yourself open to making something to share: a story, a painting, a sweater, a cake. And laugh a little.

- Andira

Introduction

When I was a kid, I remember my parents had a giant book of bedtime stories. There were 365 of them in this book and every night, they would read me one. This went on for a few years and I sincerely looked forward to hearing those stories before drifting off to sleep. Often, my dreams were influenced by the story I'd just heard. About five years ago, after publishing my fifth or sixth collection of short stories, it dawned on me that if someone wanted to, they could have created a book of 365 of my stories and done the same thing to their kid. The horror. Imagine a young impressionable child being subjected to these stories night after night for a year. What kind of a sociopath would be created? Does this mean that because you're older and jaded, you'll fare any better? I certainly hope not.

Contents

first story

As an author, every story you write is like a part of you. Like one of your children. Disappointing, underachieving children. If you think I'm going to single out any of them out to be "first," you're crazy. I wouldn't do it to the rest of them. I just couldn't.

And if you're getting a smug look on your face and thinking that the second story is really the "first" story, you can wipe that look right off. Once you read the next story, you'll see what I mean.

It screams "second story."

the bizarre

Am I guilty of a little anthropomorphism when it comes to insects?

Sure.

Am I guilty of assuming everybody knows what anthropomorphism is?

You betcha.

For those of you who don't, anthropomorphism is attributing human characteristics to other things. In this case, insects. I would stop here to make fun of what a dimwit you are, but I know what the next sentence is going to be, so I can't really be throwing stones.

There is truly a part of me that believes that millions and millions of years ago, all bugs had a head, two arms, and two legs (what did I tell you?). This was before diversity was a thing. They were tiny but they looked very much like we do. My apologies to those who don't have two arms and/or two legs (if you don't have a head, I don't think an apology is going to cut it).

Then along came evolution.

I picture evolution as a big sprawling market, equal parts bazaar and trade show. Countless exhibits where insects marched up and down, looking at evolutionary options.

Front and center would be the Wings booth. Very glitzy. Lots of traffic. "What would it take to put you into these wings today?"

"How big you want them?"

"Retractable or fixed?"

Moths so excited by their purchase, they forget the instruction manual. Flies having yet to stop by... but Wings knowing it was juuuuuust a matter of time.

Exoskeletons are also swarmed.

Antenna. Segmented Eyes. Mandibles. All open for business. The place is hopping.

Hopping. Obviously Hopping is in attendance.

Ironically, not many insects find Camouflage. Location, location, location.

You can see the gullible slug getting roped into the Slime pitch. Even the salesperson there is shocked that they make the sale.

Fresh from having sand kicked in the collective face by another beetle species, the rhinoceros beetle makes a beeline for Strength. You can bet bees took note of how it got where it wanted to go.

All the bugs starting to give the Odors booth a wide berth as they begin spraying samples on innocent passersby, like they do at the perfume counter at the mall.

In a dark alley, well off the main thoroughfare, a dung beetle storms away from the Proboscis booth yelling, "Hell no! I have my pride!" before a mosquito standing behind it slides up, looks over both shoulders, leans in and in a hushed voice says, "I just got wings. Tell me a bit more about this spear of yours."

A spider sits in front of Appendages, explaining its issue. "It's taking forever building these webs with just four limbs."

"I've got just the thing for you," comes the reply.

Little does the Appendages team know, but they'll be headed home early, centipedes stopping by a little later and cleaning them out.

"What the fuck are they going to do with all those legs? Never mind, we made quota and then some. Time to celebrate!"

The guy in Stings closes a deal and adds, "For a small upcharge… let's talk toxins."

Someone sitting behind a folding table loaded with tchotchke asking "Interested in a life under water?"

Sadly, for insects anyway, Opposable Thumbs never shows up. A flat on the way over and then a long wait for someone to arrive and change the tire forever alters the food chain as we know it. They would have done it themselves but, as their wives likes to say, they are "All thumbs."

Imagine how different the world would be if that particular tire hadn't driven over that exact sharp object. Really, a game-changer from an evolutionary perspective.

A lot of insects pass the Thanatosis and Autotomy booths without stopping, too embarrassed to inquire as to what those words mean. The folks manning them getting frustrated and yell, "I told you nobody would know what it is!" at each other. Tempers flare.

Am I guilty of assuming you also don't know what thanatosis and autotomy are and are too embarrassed to admit it?

Yep.

Perhaps I should end this by asking if I am guilty of a little insectapomorphism when it comes to people.

0 baby!

There is nothing that fills a traveler with more dread as he or she is about to depart on a long flight than seeing a mother holding a baby at the gate.

Yesterday, I was that traveler.

Everyone around the boarding area shared my apprehension. The tension was palatable.

Yes. Palatable. Not palpable.

Well yes, it was palpable, but it was also at an acceptable level. Relax, word Nazi!

Anyway, once we boarded, it soon became clear that the baby was not going to be palatable after all.

He started to cry. And cry. And cry.

He was crying and crying and crying and crying and crying and crying and crying and crying and crying and crying and crying and crying (are you reading each and every crying?) and crying and crying and crying and crying and crying and crying and crying and crying and crying and crying and crying and crying (you'd better be) and crying and crying and crying and crying and crying and crying and crying and crying and crying and crying and crying and crying (otherwise you won't be able to fully appreciate what happens next) and crying.

By the third hour, the mood was getting grim. People were turning and openly glaring.

I believe it had something to do with the change in air pressure and the effect it had on the baby's inner ear. That's why you don't see many babies on submarines.

I finally joined the myriad of angry faces turning to look at the demon-child and I swear for a second, the baby's face was as red as a beet and his eyes were black as coal and flames licked out of his quivering maw. I rubbed my eyes and he quickly returned to being all pink and cheruby.

Cheruby? You're really going to call me on that not being a word? Sorry, but he looked cheruby, so I'm going to call him cheruby; you can take your dictionary and stick it.

When I felt that nobody on board could stand a single minute more of wailing, the mother simply put her hand on the top of her baby's head, her thumb pressed firmly against his nose, and gave his head a quick twist.

A soft cracking noise was heard throughout the plane. Like a dry twig being snapped.

Suddenly, all was quiet. Then, like the end of an 80's movie, passengers, one by one, started to clap until the noise swelled and one would have thought that the mom had just sunk a fifteen-foot putt to win the Mayakoba Golf Classic in Playa del Carmen (I'm trying to reconnect with Mexican readers after calling Mexico a shithole so many times).

Still thinking about the "that's why you don't see many babies on submarines" comment, aren't you? Can't just move past it like a reader of one of the mindless feel-good books pimped by Oprah, can you? Please don't email a list of the real reasons you don't see many babies on submarines; I simply don't care. I just described a baby being murdered on an airplane flight and you're hung up on something trivial.

I was actually going to mention a baby's head imploding at a particular crush depth (like a cheruby tin can) but figured I might be pushing it if I described two infant deaths in one story. I bet you don't even appreciate my sensitivity.

Anyway, I was just wrapping up telling the person seated next to me how my sister would always carry a little bag filled with pepper on every flight so that after she got off the plane, she could induce a giant sneeze and clean out all of the bad recirculated air out of her lungs but then she got addicted and now can't even have pepper with her meals, when I saw the stewardess walking by, collecting trash before we landed.

I went to toss in my empty plastic cup when I saw two little cheruby feet sticking up out of the bag. I didn't even dare look at the mother for fear I'd see her on her phone trying to sell a stroller on eBay. I felt so weird dropping my cup on top of the formerly-bouncing-but-now-not-so-much baby corpse. Then I remembered the idiom "The tantrums of toddlerhood are all part of life's rich pageant," and stopped feeling anything.

I didn't want to be a baby.

Olive Garden of Eden

It was midway through the apple pie, served by a waitress wearing a large button among many others on her vest, that read "Experience, Not Innocence" (the letters of these three words forming the shape of a serpent) , that the words escaped her lips. Almost offhandedly.

"I just don't want to hurt you."

As soon as he heard that, he was counting the seconds until he could leave. He smiled and laughed and pretended to listen but all he wanted was out.

He could already feel the night air on his face and when he finally was able to push open the door to the Olive Garden and escape, the breeze did not disappoint.

He knew he'd never see her again.

She didn't suspect, so for a few minutes, for the first time in their rocky relationship, he knew something that she didn't.

She got into her car and he watched her drive away. The most poignant moment of any teen movie. Except, he couldn't help but fuck it up.

He saw himself in front of the car, holding up a boombox like John Cusack in *Say Anything*. Peter Gabriel's *"In Your Eyes"* blaring out.

He tried to just watch her drive away but he couldn't even get that right.

She accelerated. The John Cusack-version of him stood motionless, boombox still overhead, and tried to stare through the glare of headlights and find her eyes, as if to say, "I want to heal you."

His eyes found hers and her eyes said, "I want to kill you."

The car got closer and still he didn't move, her eyes saying, "I'm sick of feeling like a shitty person," to which his eyes replied, "so stop being a shitty person." And then, the car hit him.

He watched her driving away and he felt every bone breaking, the weight of the car rolling over him, ripping his skin, the hair on his head being unceremoniously torn off. He heard the crunching and squishing noises and smelled the odor of gasoline and tasted oil and blood in his mouth.

He stood motionless. Overwhelmed. The weight of the moment rolling over him. The back of her head looked so tiny now. Then it was only the car in the distance. Brake lights like glowing red eyes.

Then, she was gone.

Somehow, the boombox had survived.

"Love... I get so lost, sometimes...

Days pass and this emptiness fills my heart"

He didn't want to know the details of "I just don't want to hurt you." There were no good scenarios. Eve was leaving the Garden with the knowledge of those unoriginal sins and he was leaving the Garden without it, but leaving just the same.

Impossibly, the John Cusack-version of him was getting to his feet and brushing himself off.

"And all my instincts, they return...

And the grand facade, so soon will burn"

"Jesus, why can't I just have a normal heartbreaking moment?" he asked the night.

"Does that damn boombox play any other song?" he asked the John Cusack-version of himself.

"Love, I don't like to see so much pain...

So much wasted and this moment keeps slipping away"

"I guess that's a no," he said to nobody, as John had departed as well.

Butterfield's birthday

Like any conscientious dog owner, when his dog took a crap on their nightly walk around the neighborhood, Ned scooped up and deposited it in the little bag he'd brought for just such an occasion before the first fly even knew the transaction had taken place. Typically, he'd finish the walk clutching the bag, but because he was friendly with the neighbor whose lawn his dog had done his business on, he decided instead to just pop it into their garbage can which sat at the end of the driveway awaiting pick-up the following morning to save himself the unpleasantness associated with walking around clutching a bag of smelly dog excrement.

He lifted the lid and was greeted by a balloon.

Not just any balloon, but a festively-colored balloon with the words Happy Birthday emblazoned on it. It floated up right into Ned's face as if to say "Finally! Free at last!"

Ned grabbed it and felt his blood begin to boil. "What barbarian puts a balloon in the trash still inflated?" he thundered to himself. He immediately vowed never to be civil to that neighbor again. "There are rules, damnit. You don't just sing the birthday song, insist people blow out candles, cut a few pieces of cake, and then just walk away!" he said aloud and glared into his neighbor's dark window. "There are protocols to follow. Would you just wipe the cake off your mouth with Old Glory and then chuck it?"

He looked at the balloon and for the third time that day, wished he had his bugle handy. He wasn't sure *"Taps"* -also known as *"Butterfield's Lullaby"* or by the first line of the lyric, *"Day Is Done"*- was appropriate, but it certainly seemed so.

In July 1862, U.S. General Daniel Butterfield and his brigade were camped at Harrison's Landing, Virginia, recuperating after the Seven Days Battles near Richmond. Dissatisfied with the standard bugle call employed by the Army to indicate to troops it was time to go to sleep, Butterfield asked his brigade bugler, Private Oliver Wilcox Norton, to rework the existing bugle call used to signal the end of the day. He did and it caught on. As for the name, prior to Butterfield's bugle call, the lights-out call was followed by three drum beats, dubbed the *"Drum Taps,"* then simply *"Taps."* When Butterfield's call replaced the drum beats, soldiers referred to it as *"Taps"* anyway.

Butterfield's bugle call was officially known as *"Extinguish Lights"* in American military manuals until 1891.

Ned couldn't bring himself to just push the plucky balloon back into the garbage can and walk away. He knew that it would be bobbing up and down in the darkness, banging against the top, rustling and frustrated, and that thought would keep him awake all night.

"Damn it… I'm going to give this balloon the respect it deserves," and with that, he tied the balloon to the lid and walked home, still holding the dog poop, returning a few minutes later with his bugle and a pin.

He untied it and couldn't help but stare into his neighbor's house again and hope that the inhabitants therein would see what was going on. That they would see him with bugle in hand and feel remorse and emerge from their abode and do the right thing.

But they didn't.

So Ned played *"Taps"* right then and there, for all the neighborhood to hear and wonder about. When he was done, he took the pin in one hand and the balloon in the other. The balloon that had done its part and helped someone celebrate a special occasion. To the very best of its ability. The balloon that still tugged skyward, plenty of life and cheer still within it. It seemed to yearn for one more chorus of *"Happy Birthday."*

Tears began to stream down Ned's face. "*Day is done. Gone the sun. From the lakes. From the sky. All is well. Safely rest,*" and then he popped the balloon.

It fell limply over his hand. He lifted the trash lid and gently placed it inside.

He closed the lid.

His neighbor never did figure out why Ned was mad at him.

yard work

Standing at the entrance to the Manion estate recently, I couldn't help but admit that the grounds looked a little shabby. Not up to the expectations someone would have if they pulled into the driveway of a celebrated author such as myself.

So I did what Manions have done for generations when it comes to yardwork; I rolled up my sleeves and called a few landscaping companies to get a quote.

They were far too expensive and it looked for a brief time like I would have to figure out how my garage door opens, find the tools left by the previous owner, and actually exert myself. Luckily, I happened to be speaking to a neighbor that same week on the topic and he put me in touch with a guy he knew that did that type of labor for much less than his competitors. A couple of phone conversations later, I had sorted everything out.

A couple of days later, as I sat and watched from my office above my garage, I saw his crew roll up. One old man and one old lady.

His parents.

I swear.

Each looked well into their seventies and as they started to unload wheelbarrow after wheelbarrow of mulch and bring it up to the flowerbeds at the front of my house, I felt horrible. Absolutely terrible. How could I possibly sit there and let these two old people do all of my yard work?

It wasn't easy, let me tell you. At times, I couldn't even bring myself to look out the window and watch them.

The guy was your typical haggard old man but his wife… she was something special. Short and squat, built for such activities, she wore braces on both her ankles and knees and seemed no stranger to manual labor. She looked like a miniature Russian power lifter from back in the days when they were all doped up.

There was a lot of grunting involved.

Finally, after enough guilt had welled up inside me, I ventured downstairs to get a closer look. Proving the old adage that no good deed goes unpunished, my kindhearted gesture of bringing out a pitcher of ice-cold lemonade completely backfired. Not that they didn't enjoy it, but because I got a closer look at the old woman.

She was covered in dirt and debris and bugs. It was the bugs that got me.

They were still alive.

For reasons known only by science and whatever gods she prayed to, her skin was like flypaper. As if on cue, a gnat flew into the center of her forehead and stuck there. She didn't bat an eyelash nor did she make any attempt to remove it. It just sat there, little legs waving in the air, completely unable to extricate itself from her sweaty brow.

She continued to talk about plants or the weather or some other completely banal topic, but I couldn't hear a word she was saying. All I could do was to stare at the bug trapped on her face.

I wondered if she walked around at night amongst fireflies, would she eventually look like the universe?

There were bugs on her arms and bugs on her legs and all of them were doing the same little dance. My bottom lip began to quiver. Why didn't she feel them squirming and put them out of their misery? I wanted to get a wiffleball bat and whack her with it until they had all passed on.

Apparently, she wasn't talking about plants or the weather anymore because when I finally rejoined the conversation, I'd already agreed to pay her another $60 to clean my gutters. Just dandy! Now I had to worry about Helga or Olga or whatever the fuck her name was thundering around on my roof and possibly putting one of her cement feet through my upstairs ceiling. I swear, we'd need one of those cranes they use on high-rises to pull her out.

Luckily, that didn't happen because after only a few minutes, she fell off my roof. I say luckily because she wasn't injured. I'm not that callous.

Luckily, she landed on her husband.

He was injured. But getting injured is a man's job, after all. Not a delicate flower like Helga or Olga or whatever the fuck her name was. That flower drove the old man deep into the grass. After his son had collected him and driven him to the ER, there was still an "old man who got squashed by a Helga or Olga or whatever the fuck her name was" imprint on my lawn.

That night, I called the man and told him that I no longer needed his services. I would do what I should have done from the start- gone down to Home Depot and hired a few of the illegals that hang around there looking for work.

"Pone el mantillo en los parterres."

Maybe Helga or Olga or whatever the fuck her name was has a pet lizard that she feeds every night with all the insects stuck to her.

"Ese sería un buen final."

the receipt

"Do you want your receipt?" asked the young man behind the counter.

"No thanks," replied the older businessman.

"Are you sure?" the young man asked again.

"Yes. You can chuck it."

There was a long pause but instead of depositing the receipt into the trash as requested, the young man hesitated, looked at the receipt and then looked at the businessman. Finally he asked, "How are you going to remember what you bought?"

"I have this to remind me," the businessman said and lifted up his right hand, which held a bacon, cheese, and egg bagel. His face had a "game, set, match" look on it.

"What about when it's gone?"

A look of irritation crossed the face of the businessman but before he could offer his rebuttal, which would have include a rather graphic and unpleasant third option as to where the receipt could end up residing, the young man behind the counter continued.

"Do you remember your prom?"

Not one to back away from a squabble, the businessman took a moment to remember his prom. He only went to one: his senior year. For a moment, he forgot all about the piping hot bacon, cheese, and egg bagel clutched in his right hand and fumbled for pertinent particulars of that magical night.

"Do you remember the name of the girl you went with?" the young man inquired.

Ignoring the fact that he had no idea what the connection between his prom night and a bacon, cheese, and egg bagel could possibly be, the businessman played along.

"No," he said, "But I do remember distinctly that her dad sneezed when I was waiting for her to come downstairs. He sounded just like the blonde girl in a horror movie when she opens a closet to find her best friend hanging there with her throat slashed. I'll never forget it."

"But you did forget the name of the girl you took?" asked the young man again, careful not to sound in any way that he was gloating.

"The problem with the girl," the businessman plowed forward, eager to explain, "was that her feet were too big. She was the only girl in high school who didn't want bigger breasts but instead looked into a foot reduction."

After he was done offering this explanation, the businessman realized that it was still no reason not to remember the girl's name. "I remember her dad's name. His name was Chuck."

The two men looked at each other.

The young man slowly extended the hand holding the receipt.

The businessman took it.

a little latitude

"Finally. A challenge."

Not said out loud- not in any fashion we could hear anyway, but thought with great exuberance by a being beyond our understanding and typically portrayed in TV and film as anything from a cartoon to a giant blue Will Smith. Obviously, if this entity is beyond our understanding, it makes it hard to describe, but let's just say it's a Pan-Dimensional being that moves through time far differently than we do and has technology at its fingertips we can't even dream about.

Although we try.

At least I do.

To amuse itself, it grants us wishes. The vast majority of which require nothing more than zipping back in time a few thousand years, manipulating some DNA here and there, or perhaps the banking system before creating yet another reality in a multiverse that is already choked with possible outcomes.

Child's play really, if you're this Pan-Dimensional being.

But every now and then, a wish comes down the pike that the aforementioned finds interesting. Because said entity does not experience time as we do, it appears to anyone getting a wish granted that it only takes a second, a snap of the fingers or blink of an eye, for the wish to happen. What they don't realize is that once they've stated their wish, time as they know it stops and this "genie" then has to get to work on figuring how to grant the wish. This could take hundreds of "years," as we experience them, as the "afreet" has to engineer an outcome that will meet the lofty expectations of the wisher.

Making people rich or famous is so easy and mundane that this Pan-Dimensional being has often thought about taking those options completely off the table. Same with physical beauty or athletic prowess. They just don't get its toes to tapping... if it had any. I realize I muddied those particular waters earlier by referencing fingertips that it actually doesn't possess, but I trust you'll forgive me when this is all said and done.

Anyway, every now and then, a wish comes along that has the "jinni" working a bit overtime. A wish that will have your mind putting in a little extra effort if you dare try and picture it (Dare! Dare!).

Here it is… Celeste, from Akron, Ohio asked for the following: a world where things were different at the equator. On one side of the line, it was twelve hours different from the other. If it was noon south of the equator, it would be midnight on the northern side.

The Pan-Dimensional being got a chubby at this idea and Celeste wasn't even done with the wish.

On top of that, if it were summer south of the line, it would be winter on the northern side.

The Pan-Dimensional being got dizzy at the very thought of the physics involved in this wish. Even with all the resources at its disposal, it would be millennia before it could figure out how to grant this one. Obviously, E can forget all about equaling mc2. It allowed itself to imagine the finished product. Standing at the equator, a full-blown night sky to the left while the sun sat high in the sky on his right. Feeling the heat to its right and the chill to the left. Watching a cloud drift through the mid-day sky, then slide over to darkness. Eclipses... holy shit. Its head would have swam, if it had one.

Throwing out all the science surrounding hemispheres and timelines and starting again. Latitudes and longitudes tossed to the wayside. Gravity be damned!

The most difficult wish ever asked for and maybe the most spectacular. Completely selfless on the face of it, the PD entity broke one of the cardinal wish-granting rules and felt compelled to ask Celeste why she'd wished for this.

"Because," she replied, "I once asked someone I cared about to try and imagine it and he wouldn't."

The powerful-beyond-measure being wanted so badly to ask another question, just a quick "Why?!" but it had already broken one cardinal rule and it didn't want to push its luck. It went to work.

A second later, Celeste was standing on the equator she'd always wanted to stand on.

Now it's up to you to picture it. A sky split in half between light and dark. Details matter, especially at sunrise/sunset and during storms.

And then come up with a "Why?!" that works for you. I'm asking a lot, I know, but keep in mind, I'll give you a little latitude.

a halo is merely a hat that lets the rain in

Whenever you face a difficult decision or are called upon to figure out a complicated problem, you're often advised to "put on your thinking cap."

I don't own such a cap.

At the drop of a hat, it now jumps to the top of my to-do list.

I realize, of course, that this is a metaphor (this realization coming even without the requisite headgear), but when I thought about it (again without the necessary chapeau), I realized that having something on my head might actually improve my cognitive abilities.

> *"Why should anyone be frightened by a hat?"*
> -Antoine de Saint-Exupéry, *The Little Prince*

You might be wondering to yourself if I am currently wearing anything on my head as I write this.

Obviously not.

But don't let that stop you from A) continuing to read this, and B) considering acquiring a thinking cap of your own. Were you to be wearing such a hat, you might even be getting more out of this.

Probably not, though. It would have to be a pretty big fucking hat for that to be the case.

A sombrero perhaps. Your thinking sombrero. Like they wear in ol' Mexico. If memory serves, in old westerns, there were always a bunch of Mexicans wearing sombreros leaning against dilapidated buildings, sound asleep. For years, I wrote this off as laziness.

Perhaps they were all just lost in thought. Perhaps Mexico is a paradise for thinkers.

"I think, therefore I sleep, amigo."

> *"Everywhere you hang your hat is home.*
> *Home is the bright cave under the hat."*
> \- Lance Morrow

Does a thinking cap have to be tied to your ethnicity?

Is it a thinking beret in France?

"I recommend the French beret, for it gives the impression of just the right soft toughness, a veritable wave of sophisticated brain matter. It is the kind of hat that inspires a person to grow into it, to become the person they never knew they could be. The space between the top of the head and the beginnings of hat is among the most intimate of areas: earlobe behinds, elbow insides, and anuses. One must pay heed to such spaces for they hold a potential not fully known (but generally agreed to be vast)."

-Meia Geddes, *Love Letters to the World*

A thinking ushanka in Russia?

Do Moroccan's reach for their thinking fez?

What about cowboys? Is it a ten-gallon thinking cap?

Makes you wonder about graduates tossing their mortarboards into the air after they receive their degrees. Is this too a metaphor? As if announcing they're done thinking?

Got you thinking there, didn't I? (Perhaps wishing there was a certain something perched on top of your head?)

"You can put it on and say, "Hey you, person without a hat! I've got something you don't!

"How did I get it? Probably by being worth more to society."
- Alice LeGrow

Jews are renowned for their intellect… could it be the 24/7 thinking yarmulkes?

If that's the case, why doesn't it work for men who wear toupees?

What's the difference between a German thinking pickelhaube and this story?

The pickelhaube has a point.

(A tip of the cap to you if you got that.)

"Hang on to your hat. Hang on to your hope.
And wind the clock, for tomorrow is another day."
-E. B. White

the super gay story

(my contribution to the anthology *Stories My Gay Uncle Told Me*)

My mother has three brothers. They're all gay. She describes their gayness in similar terms as the porridge in *Goldilocks and the Three Bears*. It's impossible to tell that one of her brothers is gay. You can tell another brother is gay but only if you pay attention. The third brother, the one she calls Aunt Steve, is wildly, over-the-top gay. Super-gay.

I remember the first time I met my aunt. It was as if he was worried everyone in the restaurant wouldn't know they were dining with a gay man in the building. He was wearing a shawl that looked like it could have been stolen from his grandmother and he squealed a lot when he talked. By the time he ordered his meal, even the cooks knew there was a gay man in attendance.

Aunt Steve was the best.

One summer, I went to stay with him for a few days. He lived on a quiet cul-de-sac , which he told me was a metaphor for his love life. At the time, I didn't understand the reference but I do remember he got a very faraway look in his eyes as he said it. His house wasn't anything like I imagined it would be. I expected pink leather sofas and orange shag carpet. Instead, it looked like every other home I'd ever been in. I was a little deflated and I told him as much.

Then, he told me a story about trying to fit in. A story I will retell to my children when they're old enough to understand… and I fully understand it myself.

At one time, Aunt Steve did have a pink leather sofa and all of the other garish things I was expecting from my super-gay relation. The problem was that none of his neighbors would ever come to visit because the contents of his super gay house made them uncomfortable.

Even people going door to door to talk about the Lord or selling cookies to raise money for Little League started skipping his house.

Even his two gay brothers apparently had something to say about his décor.

"Want to know what I did?" he asked me.

"Of course," I replied.

Apparently, every year, everyone in the cul-de-sac would hold a joint garage sale. They would all chip in to publicize it and it became something of a tradition. There were fourteen families taking part that fateful Sunday morning.

"The night before, I arranged to have six workers meet at my house early in the morning."

My head swam as I listened. What super-gay thing could Aunt Steve possibly have planned?

"The garage sale was scheduled to open at seven-thirty. At seven twenty-nine, I strode up the driveway of my closest neighbor and made an offer on all of his stuff."

I can't be entirely sure, but I'm guessing my eyes shone as I listened.

"'I'll take it!' I announced to my shocked neighbor. 'I'll pay whatever is on the little sticky tags. Deal?' I asked him."

At this point, I'm entirely sure my eyes were glistening. I had no idea where this was going, but I loved it.

"He was shocked. He didn't know what to say. My six workers marched up and began bringing the complete contents of his driveway into my house. Furniture, dishes, old board games. You name it."

No one could tell a story like Aunt Steve.

"I then went to each and every house in the cul-de-sac and bought up their offerings. One after another. After a few houses, they began to see what was happening and met me on the sidewalk. There was no bartering or squabbling. Fourteen houses in a row. I bought it all. They didn't know what to make of me."

He sat back and smiled at the memory. I looked down at the couch I was sitting on. I looked over to the side table and then across to the kitchen chairs. A lightbulb went off.

"That's right. Everything you see in here is from my neighbors. I was able to replace everything."

The realization of what he was saying hit me like a ton of bricks. I didn't know how to feel. Was this a story of fitting in or surrendering? He saw the confusion on my face. Sensed I was wrestling with something big.

"Before you ask me if they started to come over and visit more, let me finish." There was a little squeal in his voice. "After everything was in my house, I had the six workers take out all of my existing stuff and put it on my driveway. I had already priced everything and it was ready to sell."

I leaned in further, captivated to hear the exciting conclusion.

"Let me tell you, it was a feeding frenzy!" Aunt Steve threw up his hands in glee. "I mean, where else could you get a Mauro Oliveira Decorated Chair for fifteen dollars or a Manchester Gay Pride Doodle Map Cushion for fifty cents? The crowds that love garage sales were just showing up and my neighbors no longer had anything to do but take a look. It was pandemonium!"

"Fifteen dollars? Fifty cents?" I thought to myself. I thought this was a story of revenge or at least breaking even. I was feeling a bit crestfallen.

As if answering my unasked question, he continued. "It wasn't about making money. I lost hundreds of dollars. Everything I owned was scooped up for pennies on the dollar that day." He paused dramatically. "Just like everyone else."

Slowly, a smile crept across my face.

"So, it doesn't matter if they come to visit me. I know that my 'Peter Getting Out of Nick's Pool' print hangs above the fireplace directly across the street."

Goldilocks be damned, Aunt Steve was just right.

the moth

Some might categorize it as a youthful indiscretion. Some of his peers called it pyromania. The court-appointed psychologist called it an impulse control issue.

Whatever you call it, the abandoned building burned to the ground just the same. The best hour of his life.

You never know when you look at someone what they're carrying around inside them.

The only poem he ever wrote was in high school. It was a response to a homework question, "What is fire?" Perhaps his teacher got a glimpse into what he was carrying around when he read "An Ode to Combustion."

Although unexpectedly beautiful, it did not include the word "pyre" (So obvious! It rhymes with fire). An oversight that haunts him to this day. If he could go back and change things, this would be second on his list. After, of course, burning that building down.

So, he made changes in his life. Improvements. *Nosce te ipsum* and such.

He owns an electric stove. In his fireplace sits one of those plastic logs and fake fire things. When he turns it on, orange and yellow "flames" roll endlessly on a loop above the logs.

It provides no heat.

Neither does his social life. Every Halloween, he goes as a moth. This allows him a good reason to approach girls that are smoking. How he approaches them, with the same flight plan and erratic gesticulations of a moth, leaves much room for improvement.

His moth costume, with its numerous small, round burn marks, bears witness to this.

Masturbation offers him little comfort. Instead, during wildfire season, he'll often takes days off work just to sit and watch the *Weather Channel's* coverage. "California... all those expensive homes. Mmmm."

When he explained to co-workers how he spent his vacation, one of them jokingly asked if he was crazy. "Where there's smoke, there's fire," snickered a plump woman in earshot.

"Sometimes," he replied, "there is fire without smoke. In complete combustion, if there is enough oxygen present, the burning fuel will produce only water and carbon dioxide. I believe you're thinking of incomplete combustion, where there isn't enough oxygen and carbon and carbon monoxide are also released, i.e. smoke."

Nobody said a word. Before it got awkward, he added, "There may be a great fire in our soul, yet no one ever comes to warm himself at it, and the passers-by see only a wisp of smoke." Long pause. "Vincent van Gogh said that."

Before it got wildly awkward, he walked away.

He allows himself one exception to his many self-imposed rules. A single candle sits on his kitchen table.

Unscented, of course. Its purpose having nothing to do with making his house smell like Antique Sandalwood or Cucumber Melon.

It is always alight. He says goodbye to it when he leaves and it's there to greet him upon his return. He stares at it like an old lover. Soaking in the same chemical reaction involved in the best hour of his life. A light in the darkness. Flickering and dancing.

Why do I tell you all this? Because you never know when you look at someone what they're carrying around inside them.

"The moth takes off again, and we both step back, because he's circling at eye level now and seems to have lost rudder control, smacking into the wall on each round. He circles lower and lower, spinning around the candle in tighter revolutions, like a soap sud over an open drain. A few times he seems to touch the flame, but dances off unhurt.

Then he ignites like a ball of hair, curling into an oily puff of fumes with a hiss. The candle flame flickers and dims for a moment, then burns as bright as before.

> *"Moth smoke lingers."*
> -Mohsin Hamid, *Moth Smoke*

milk carton kid

(first appeared on the *creepypasta.com* website)

"So, why are you here?" she asked.

Pretty standard opening for a psychologist sitting down with a patient for the first time. She was young, pretty, and Shahrokh (an unnecessarily ethnic name) immediately felt comfortable in her presence.

"Well, before I launch into what's been happening recently, I think I'd better start at the beginning."

The therapist smiled in agreement. She leaned back in her chair and opened a small notebook.

"You see, over twenty years ago, I had a second cousin named Alice (You think I'm going with another ethnic name? Think again.). A beautiful little girl. I met her when she was two."

The surprisingly unethnic-looking man fidgeted in his seat, unsure how to continue.

"The first time I met her was at a restaurant. We were seated at opposite ends of the table and her parents, my cousins, kept feeding her these little animal crackers to keep her happy. She would either eat them or try to hand them back and make a game out of it. Adorable."

Shahrokh (Yeah, that name is a mouthful and it sort of makes you think that the animal crackers only came in the shape of a cow. A change might have to be made.) leaned over and picked up his bottle of water and took a swig.

"Then, her parents told us to watch as she did a trick. We did. 'Do your magic trick,' they said to her. Alice got a big grin and said 'Majjj'…

that was how she pronounced magic." The way Shahrokh (ok, well, clearly this name was a mistake. Let's just call him Tim from now on.) said it made the psychologist laugh despite herself. When he heard the laugh, Tim felt a weird sensation but continued the story.

"They put one of the animal crackers in her little hand. 'Majjj,' she said and closed it. Everyone leaned in and Alice was thrilled to have everyone paying attention to her. She opened her hand and the animal cracker was gone and everyone at the table clapped and hooted and hollered their approval."

(Shahrokh would never have said "hooted and hollered"… he was killing the story. Tim, on the other hand, had no problem saying it.)

"That's cute," said the therapist.

"Yeah, it was. She kept doing it through the course of the evening and everyone was having a great time. The problem was I couldn't see *how* she was doing it. Everyone just assumed she was dropping the cracker but when I looked under the table, there were no crackers on the floor. I looked on her lap and saw nothing. Her arms were bare so there was no place to stash a cracker and I watched her parents closely to see if they were complicit in the trick but they seemed innocent enough."

After jotting down a few key parts of the story in her notebook, the therapist asked, "So where were the crackers going?"

"I don't know. I really didn't know. It seemed like I was the only one who actually didn't get the trick or noticed that the crackers were actually disappearing. I felt a little like a fool, to be honest."

Tim took a short breath in. "A few days later, I volunteered to babysit Alice. I hate to admit it but I had an ulterior motive. I wanted to find out where the crackers were going. How she did it. Only minutes after her parents closed the door behind them, I had a box of crackers out and was sitting in front of her asking her to do her majjj. She did. Again and again."

"And? Did you figure out the trick?" asked the therapist.

"No. Alice would just laugh and say 'majjj' and the damn cracker would disappear. She did it with anything that would fit into her hand. She disappeared bottle caps and coins and an eraser. It freaked me out."

More note jotting by the therapist. "Interesting," was all she said.

"I know it sounds crazy."

She stopped jotting. "Crazy isn't a word I use a lot," she replied, smiling.

"You haven't heard why I'm here." He wanted to say it lightheartedly but the small chuckle he planned on adding at the end died in his throat.

"Alice disappeared two weeks later." It took a few moments for him to continue. "She was never found. Just gone. It wrecked everybody."

The therapist automatically reached for the box of Kleenex in a well-rehearsed gesture. "I'm so sorry," she said.

Tim sobbed but kept trying to continue. The first few attempts were swallowed up with grief.

Eventually… "I was in the supermarket months later and I saw her picture on the side of a carton of milk…"

More sobbing. Primal and raw.

"I fucking bought it and brought it home and it's still in my refrigerator. How can I throw it out? I didn't even drink the milk. I just poured it out when it went bad." Tim's hands were balled up in tight fists.

"Breathe. Take your time," was all the therapist could say.

When he was finally able to calm down a bit, he carried on, head down. "Here's the crazy part… the last few nights, I've been hearing someone in my kitchen and then in the morning, when I walk in, I find a single animal cracker on the table."

He looked up slowly at her. "I'm too much of a coward to go see who's there. I'm just so sacred I'll walk in and see a little girl standing there and shit my pants. Or, I'll walk into an empty kitchen and open the refrigerator door to get a drink and when I close it, Alice will be standing there and I'll stand there frozen or I'll shit my pants."

He fumbled in his pocket and then produced an animal cracker.

"What's going on?" he finally asked the therapist.

She leaned forward and opened her hand. He placed the animal cracker in it. She closed her hand and when she opened it, the cracker was gone.

"Majjj."

I realized I never gave the therapist a name. Let's call her… Alice.

well-done

"Here's the problem I've been having with your establishment," the man began in a calm and even tone. Before him, stood an earnest young woman holding a small notepad, seemingly eager to take his order in a timely fashion.

What onlookers, if there were any (which there weren't), might not know is that this was not the first time this particular man had begun this particular conversation at that particular diner. If he'd begun attempting to let a waitress know how he would like his hash browns prepared one time, he'd done it a dozen.

"I always order my hash browns well-done and every time they are presented to me, they are in fact not well-done. Every single solitary time. No matter how much I beg and plead during the ordering phase, I'm still presented with hash browns that are the furthest thing from well-done."

The young lady shifted her weight from one foot to the other and said, "So, you want them well-done?"

"No. I want them extraordinarily well-done. The wellest-done that this eatery has ever prepared."

"Ok," the waitress replied, then added, "I will tell the chef to make sure they are well-done," with a reassuring nod of her head.

The man, clearly not satisfied with this, continued. "I have heard these very promises a number of times from individuals just as sincere as yourself and have yet to have been satisfied with the end results. Please allow me to elaborate about how I would like my hash browns prepared."

Not seeing an option, the woman shifted her weight back to the original foot and gave the man her undivided attention.

"When you place the order, I want you to tell the chef to put my hash browns on the grill and then walk away and forget about them completely. Go do his taxes or pick up his kids from school. Put them entirely out of his mind until such a time as the smell of burning hash browns reaches his nose. It's at this moment I need you to spring into action and restrain him. Do not allow him to approach my hash browns. It is imperative that you do whatever is necessary to keep him away from the grill. Even as my hash browns are engulfed in flames, I want you to whisper in his ear, 'They are *almost* done…. just not yet,' and keep him from applying his spatula to my precious shredded potato side dish. He will struggle and use profanity, but hold him you must. Thick black smoke will begin to pour out of the kitchen and the fire department will be summoned, yet you must do whatever it takes to keep my hash browns on the grill a little longer. Every second counts."

The man paused, having delivered the previous monologue without the benefit of a breath of air.

He then resumed after a long inhale and exhale.

"News helicopters should be circling the diner before the fire chief finally removes my hash browns from the grill. Do you now truly understand exactly how well-done I want my hash browns?" the man inquired.

"Really well-done?" the waitress offered hopefully.

"Yes. You've hit the nail on the head. Well-done."

(One hour later)

"This is Sarah Johnson reporting from the scene of a local fire. Behind me you can see the charred and still smoldering remains of Lucky's Diner."

The camera pans back and forth across the blackened structure and the parking lot filled with curious onlookers. And one man sitting on the curb with a plate in front of him. On that plate sits something charcoal black. It is impossible to tell what exactly it is.

The man tucks his napkin under his chin, produces a fork from his pocket, and smiles broadly.

Dr. Fart

Dr. Fart is a clinical psychologist. Fart is not his real name; it is a moniker given to him by his patients due to his unique approach to therapy.

In a nutshell, he believes that we communicate a lot of information about ourselves through our anus. Happy farts, those that sound like a clown's horn, rarely smell bad. The terrible odors usually result from farts that sound like a hiss or emit no sound at all.

He has the worst-smelling office in the city.

One day, a man walked in and plopped down on his couch. He immediately launched into a story.

"A few weeks ago, I bought a virtual reality headset… to play games on. I was excited to see what new technology was out there. It was fantastic. I put it on and played for hours."

Dr. Fart began to scribble down pertinent details. He encouraged the man to continue with a quick "So, what brought you here?"

"The problem was, when I finally took the headset off, I was standing in a park. Two blocks away from my house."

"I see," replied Dr. F.

"When I walked back to my house, across a busy road I might add, my front door was closed. I know I didn't open any doors in my game."

More scribbling from Dr. F. "How do you explain that?" he asked.

"I can't. It seems impossible. Every time I played a game with the VR goggles, I ended up outside of my house. I thought it might be a defective headset, so I returned it and got a new one. Didn't help. I thought it might be the game, so I played a different one. Same thing happened. I began to lock my front door when I played, but I still ended up outside. Only difference was that when I walked back to the house, I had to enter through a window."

"A window, you say?" inquired the good doctor.

"Yes. I had to break into my own house."

"I see. How do you explain this?"

The question frustrated the man. "I can't. That's why I'm here."

"I see," said Dr. Fart. "Perhaps this is a question for a physicist down at the college. Or maybe the manufacturer of the headset could be contacted."

"I've tried both, doctor. They couldn't explain it either. The real problem, aside from the physical danger I might be in crossing busy streets while I'm completely oblivious to the world around me, is that the other day, I ended up in a convenience store. When I took off the headset, there were a bunch of people standing around, staring at me."

"I bet that was a bit embarrassing," speculated Dr. Fart.

"That wasn't the worst part. I was so embarrassed, I quickly put the headset back on."

"Hmmmm," contributed Dr. F.

"And in the game I was playing, I was suddenly surrounded by people staring at me as well."

"Interesting. Really interesting." Eventually Dr. Fart felt the need to speak again as the silence that followed began to get uncomfortable. "You are aware that I am called Dr. Fart by my regular clientele, correct?"

"No. I was unaware of that. I just looked up the nearest therapist to my house. That explains a few things though," the man added as he wrinkled up his nose. He felt a sudden burst of sympathy for the couch he was sitting on.

"Yes. I am Dr. Fart. What I'm going to need you to do, before we make any progress on this rather fascinating situation, is make another appointment for next week. An hour before our scheduled time, I'll need you to eat a family-sized can of baked beans. Beans contain a lot of raffinose, which is a complex sugar that the body has trouble digesting. When it passes through the small intestines into the large intestines, bacteria breaks it down, producing hydrogen, carbon dioxide, and methane gas, which has no choice but to exit through the rectum. Wash it all down with a large glass of milk and we can get to work on your problem."

"Ok then. I'll see you next week," said the man, waving cordially as he departed.

With that, he took off the headset.

It was a beautiful day to be at the park.

Thelma without a Louise (the big sleep)

Thelma looked a lot like Louise from the movie *Thelma and Louise*, if Louise had aged a few years and let herself go a bit.

The trouble with telling you about her is that it will seem in some way I am endorsing her worldview.

I am not.

I am simply telling you something Thelma believes. Something she puts into practice to the annoyance of all around her. Which explains why there is not a Louise in Thelma's life.

Not that she is a lesbian. I am referring to a close friend whom you'd feel comfortable driving off the edge of a cliff with.

And just because I reference that scene in the movie in no way means I'm endorsing it. I've never seen it. I will never see it. I just know that it ends with them both hurtling off a cliff for some reason.

I guess I should have given you a spoiler alert but if you haven't gotten around to watching *Thelma and Louise* by now, I'm guessing you never will. It came out in friggin' 1991.

So what is this "worldview" I mentioned earlier? (I can sense I'm starting to lose you with all the *Thelma and Louise* nonsense- that's what makes me the writer I am… an uncanny knack of knowing when I'm losing readers. I should know by now; I've lost of thousands of them.)

Thelma sincerely believes she's helping by going to sleep when someone she knows is having something unpleasant done to them- surgery, cavities filled, that type of stuff.

Why does she believe she's helping?

Because when she wakes up, it's over with for the person.

I'm going to give you a minute to wrestle with that one. Her friends and family went through the same type of mental gymnastics the first time she explained it to them.

After explaining it to them, she expected them to thank her.

"I had to sleep through the whole afternoon just to get you here safe and sound," she elucidated to her befuddled sister who was recovering from a gall bladder operation. Her sister, still fuzzy from the drugs, hung up on her.

Honestly, I wish I would have thought to name her sister Louise. That would have been perfect. Especially given the upcoming ending. You would have said to yourself, "Wow, that Manion can sure spin a yarn that makes you think."

Now? The usual: "Fuckin' Manion."

Although her circle of friends slowly decreased through the years, Thelma still had plenty of reasons to sleep. It got to the point where she would read about people going through turmoil of one type or another in the newspaper and she would march into the nearest pharmacy and stock up on sedatives.

"I want to help," she would tell the disinterested pharmacist behind the counter.

"And you do, Thelma. That will be $49.50," he would reply disinterestedly.

I don't think Thelma was crazy. I just don't think she knew what else to do. Empathy is a slippery slope.

"*Was* crazy?" you might be asking yourself. "Since when is this muddled excuse for a story in the past tense?"

Maybe compassion and logic and our seemingly limitless ability to rationalize things make for a bad cocktail.

"Don't ignore your reader, Manion!" you're probably saying out loud at this point. Maybe not. I like to pretend you're really invested in these words.

So anyway… Thelma, realizing that there is so much sadness and suffering in the world, the only way to bring it to an end was to get into her 2017 Honda Accord and drive to the limestone quarry near the mall (you know the one. "Oh right... the *limestone* quarry."). So she did. She slowly drove through the fence- it gave way surprisingly easy (a nearby spider rolled its eight eyes and said, "So much for your advanced technology. So much for steel.") - and then all the way to the edge.

"Oh shit…" you're no doubt saying to yourself now. A lump in your throat.

Thelma called her sister and said "You're welcome," then hit the gas.

fugit inreparabile tempus

You know who I respect? There are a few flies that hang around my outside trashcan the same way I imagine young toughs would hang around pool rooms in the 50's. If they wore t-shirts, I'm certain there would be a pack of smokes rolled up on one of their six sleeves.

You pictured that, didn't you?

You love that nostalgic stuff.

The reason I respect them so much is that unlike the swarms of other flies that visit my yard on a given day, they're waiting for me.

They know the routine.

After dinner every night, I walk out with a bag of garbage. I walk up to the outside receptacle, open the lid, and toss in the evening's refuse. The lid is open for maybe two seconds and in those two seconds, the flies that are gathered around make their move.

In they go.

The smell of raw garbage must be intoxicating but they also know that when that lid closes, it's closed for 24 hours. There's no wandering in and out of my outside garbage can. You have to be committed.

And as they fly in, there are always a few flies on their way out. Their shift is over. They are sated and ready for some sunshine. They must hear me coming and get all excited about their coming release. If they don't pay attention or if they're feeling a bit sluggish, they get to spend another 24 hours in the hole.

My point is this: 24 hours of pitch darkness must be rough if you're a fly.

How do I know this?

By the looks on their faces when I approach the garbage can. They have that same forlorn look that you see in old black and white photos of coal miners just before they started their shifts. Except with five eyes. That's 250% more forlorn than humans are capable of being.

How do they know there isn't a spider sneaking up on them as they start tucking in?

I'm sure their imaginations run wild. The slightest rustling noise is a five-inch praying mantis about to snatch them up and eat their head.

Do they nod to each other as they pass?

"Frank." Little nod.

"There's some ham in a bag at the bottom on the left. By the shoe."

"You don't say. Thanks."

I picture them talking like flies that used to hover around pool rooms in the 50's. Maybe even with a little Brooklyn accent.

Is it sexist that I imagine female flies have no interest in my garbage can? That they are all over at a picnic in a park somewhere? Probably not a safe place for female fly anyway. All those tough flies, all that darkness. I feel like some nasty *Animal Planet* stuff would go down in my garbage can if they ended up there for a night.

When the flies I respect so much are in my completely dark garbage can, do they even fly? Are they crashing into each other? Are they cursing or are they good-natured and even gather near the top of the can after a few hours to play games of chance? Do they tell stories about the time I went on vacation for two weeks and only a few flies made it out?

"It was a friggin' nightmare. Thirteen days and nights. Temperatures outside were in the 90s. I can only imagine how hot it was in the can."

They call it "the can."

If you were one of the ones that made it out, I bet all the other flies would nod and tip the caps I imagine them wearing whenever they flew by. Wondering what they were thinking when they finally saw that strip of light at the top of the can. Were they crying their five eyes out or did they play it cool when the fresh air hit their face?

"Hey rookie! You ready for The Show? That's recyclables. There's nothing in there to eat. Come over here. Follow me in."

Tonight, I'm going to imagine all the flies as having t-shirts, caps, and Brooklyn accents. I suggest you do the same. I even left the game of chance I mentioned earlier up to you to choose. Was it cards? Was it dice? Did one of the flies drop a card and everyone else grumbled and rolled their five eyes and nobody wanted to be the one to crawl all the way down into the darkness to retrieve it?

Did you forget that it was completely dark when you selected your game of chance?

No worries. Braille cards.

(Are we really making things up for blind flies now?)

> *"And when Hugh would grow progressively Gandhi on me,*
> *I'd remind him that these were pests—disease carriers*
> *who feasted upon the dead and then came indoors*
> *to dance upon our silverware."*
> - David Sedaris, *When You Are Engulfed in Flames*

socks to be you

Putting on a sock this morning, I guess I pulled too hard or something because the bottom piece ripped clean off. It looked like I had on an anklet and the world's smallest leg warmer.

It wasn't even that old. I guess I need to buy better socks or at least put them on a bit more gingerly.

The odd thing was the reaction of the other sock.

The angst that seemed to permeate the room as I sat on the edge of the bed.

I realize it had always been part of a pair, but I couldn't put my finger on the source of its anguish. Was it scared it was going to share a similar fate, like I was some sort of wild-eyed, slavering sock murderer, or was it scared of being alone? Did it fear that as its compatriot was no longer, it would be tossed? Was it hoping somewhere there was another sock that looked almost identical so it could once again be part of a pair or did it imagine a place where people dropped off single socks so that people with only one leg wouldn't have to buy two?

I wonder if your sympathy for this sock is tied in any way to what it's made of.

I hope I don't have any anti-acrylic readers, but these days it's hard to tell. People keep their thoughts on polyester and nylon pretty much to themselves.

That doesn't mean it's right.

You know exactly what I mean; don't pretend you don't.

A sock is a sock and I hope it doesn't need to be wool or a cotton blend for you to accept it.

Don't get me started on the color of the sock. I know you have your prejudices, but let's get one thing perfectly clear: black socks are not lazy.

If anything, black and brown socks work harder than any other color. Show me a busy workplace and I will show you dark socks. Ironic, isn't it? White-collar workers wear blue socks and blue-collar workers wear white socks.

I believe the true purpose of literature is to tackle the tough topics and allow the reader to have powerful epiphanies. Unless I miss my guess, you just had one.

And not to digress too much, but is there anything more loathsome than someone who dresses very conservatively but sports "crazy" socks? Purposely crossing and uncrossing their legs at the meeting so everyone can get a peek at their "wild" socks, hoping everyone is thinking to themselves "That guy isn't as square as I thought he was." We're not.

Fuck you and your bright yellow SpongeBob socks.

I realize that only a few paragraphs ago, I was waxing poetic about the noble role of literature in society, and I apologize for the use of profanity, but those guys just make me want to punch them right in their cakeholes.

What I really feel bad for is taking away the spotlight from the single sock that started this story off on such a positive foot.

Wow. I just walked right into that pun.

Shit. There was another one.

If you took time-lapse photography of how people have worn their socks from one generation to the next, as fashions come and go, the height would bounce from the ankle up to the knee and then back down again. Up and down, up and down. Shorts seem to have an inverse relationship to socks, there's always a fixed amount of leg showing. I wonder if someone from MIT has ever created a mathematical formula for this.

You just had another epiphany, didn't you?

The truly odd thing is that you read the sentence "The odd thing was the reaction of the other sock" and kept reading. Remember the feeling you had when the premise really sunk in? "He's anthropomorphizing a sock… wow."

And now you've had two epiphanies as a result. Just goes to show.

"My socks DO match. They're the same thickness."
-Steven Wright

the ubiquity of kissing

What the hell is a kiss anyway?

In a 2015 survey, University of Nevada's anthropology department found nearly half of the 168 different cultures cluttering up the planet don't engage in pressing their mouths together as a display of affection. Apparently, the words "gross" and "icky" popped up a lot.

If you stop to consider how many different ways we come into physical contact with each other, and the dizzying number of things we try to communicate with these gestures, you might think I'm being stubborn if I hold out for a traditional kiss.

There's back-slapping, handshakes, fist-bumping, and hugs. Each with their own messages. Brushing the hair out of someone's eyes or slapping their face. Two distinct messages. Some cultures squeeze elbows and some hold hands to express intimacy.

Eskimos rub noses, also called kunik. Apparently, they do this because they're scared that if they did it with their mouths, their lips might freeze together. Given how cold it is up there, I'd be more concerned about their snot freezing together. Have you ever seen an Eskimo without a bunch of snot hanging under his or her nose? Which begs the question: do Eskimos give CPR by holding the mouth closed and blowing into the nose? It might explain why their life expectancy is lower than ours. If you're an Eskimo having a heart attack, you might want to head somewhere else. Just giving you a heads up, Nanook.

But back to lips.

They are unique, like fingerprints, and are the most sensitive part of our bodies. Not the penis nor the vagina. Not even close. There are over a million nerve-endings packed into our lips. No food or drink gets into our bodies without their say-so and the lion's share of air passes through them on its way into us. More specifically (and much more importantly), every sigh and every whisper on their way out.

But back to the nerve-endings.

Over a million of them. It would take you 11 days, 13 hours, 46 minutes, and 40 seconds just to count them all (no breaks allowed).

More than every wink, blush, subtle arching of the back, and not-so-subtle swiveling of the hips combined.

At some point, I'm sure you're waiting for me to get to the point. Ok, here goes...

> *"...I keep breaking things - appointments and porcelain,*
> *thinking of your lips ..."*
> - John Geddes, *A Familiar Rain*

Sometimes it's like there are only two things that exist in the universe: my memory and her lips. You wanted a point? There's your point.

> *"He drew her very tenderly close and their lips met*
> *like starved hearts."*
> - F. Scott Fitzgerald, *At Your Age*

Of course, that sounds so dramatic, but did I mention the one million nerve-endings?

> *"With kisses your mouth taught me... my lips came to know fire."*
> - Pablo Neruda, *Then Come Back: The Lost Neruda Poems*

Obviously, it's not just me, which provides some comfort.
(Fumbling ever-so-briefly to regain my composure.)

The color of our lips is caused by visible blood capillaries under our skin. They are visible because the lips have one of the thinnest layers of skin on the body. They never sweat, because lips do not have sweat glands. They are the only parts of the body where the inside extends to the outside. The membrane that makes up the inner lips also makes the outer lips. And, unlike our backsides, they get thinner as we age.

> *"If you kiss her cheeks, she is your friend;*
> *if you kiss her lips, she is your lover;*
> *if you kiss her heart, she is your soul mate."*
> *- Matshona Dhliwayo*

And then there's that… always that.

> *"I want a kiss that's like a huge wave crashing*
> *against a rocky shoreline.*
> *The kind with a roar, where the water shoots up*
> *and turns into mist.*
> *There's got to be a better way of saying that."*
>
> -Me

I don't think I'm being stubborn.

misfortune teller

The idea came to him as he was mowing his lawn. As he was trying to do his best to mow in straight lines while at the same time humming along with, and occasionally doing a small shimmy to, a selection of his favorite songs, at a decibel level that his phone warned him was detrimental to his long-term hearing, an enormous golden dragonfly began following him around.

Very unusual, as dragonflies weren't something that usually haunted his neighborhood. I'll explain "haunted" in a moment. It wasn't until the dragonfly's tenth or eleventh pass that he noticed it was dragonflies. Plural. No apostrophe necessary. One giant golden one and one smaller one and they seemed to be getting very amorous as they flew around completely entwined.

"What sorcery is this?" he said under his breath.

I said "haunted" earlier because his recent-ex girlfriend believes not only in coincidences but also in her ability to cause them. While she dabbled in a variety of flying insects, her specialty was dragonflies. She'd told him so on a number of occasions.

Why, he wondered, would she send a couple of sexed-up winged minions to his house when he was busy trying to forget that she had just recently rejected his sexual advances? She knew he'd taken it hard.

That's when he got his brilliant idea… although, to be fair, his morality was on shaky ground.

This girl he was infatuated with believed in all things mystical. From healing crystals and speaking to the dead to telepathy and Feng Shui, she thought all of it was as valid and reasonable as any science or psychology she'd ever heard. Included in all of that were tarot cards.

He, on the other hand, thought it was all nonsense. But the way she believed it seemed to him to be so endearing that he not only tolerated it, but her passion for it somehow made her more attractive.

He smiled ear to ear as his little scheme came together in his head. Had he not been pushing a mower, he would have no doubt rubbed his hands together and let loose a diabolical laugh.

The plan?

I thought you'd never ask.

He would get her to agree to one last date, begging if necessary. A nice goodbye where they could part friends. A pleasant meal on the nearby boardwalk. It was littered with places to eat. How could she say no? He stopped the mower briefly to rub his hands together and indulge in a quick, diabolical laugh. That's how foolproof he thought his plan was.

You see, on this boardwalk was a fortune teller. He would bring up some paranormal thing or other during the meal to set the stage and then, as they walked back to their cars, they would pass this fortune teller and he would casually suggest that before they decide to part ways for good, they should consult a higher power.

He would earnestly tell her that if the fortune teller said they should break up, he would never contact her again.

If, on the other hand, the reading suggested that perhaps she should reconsider and sleep with him, she would be duty-bound to follow through.

That catch?

And here's the part that will explain why the mower once again came to rest, allowing him to rub his hands together and let loose another diabolical laugh: he would visit the fortune teller beforehand and pay her off to ensure that his ex got exactly the reading he needed her to.

Listen, I told you right up front that the idea was on shaky ground in terms of ethics. I try not to sugarcoat things. He would argue that if you're going to turn over responsibility for your personal decisions to a tarot deck, then let the cards fall where they may. All's fair and whatnot.

Relax a little; the story isn't over yet.

If you know anything about my stories, they usually never end well for the people engaged in such shakiness. Or people not engaged in such shakiness.

So, everything went according to plan. He got his ex to accept his dinner invitation. He paid off the fortune teller. He positioned his bed centrally and out of line from the door, made sure there was a bedside table on each side of the bed, bought new sheets in soothing colors, invested in some candles, and adjusted the mirror so it couldn't be seen from the bed. He Feng Shuid the shit out of his bedroom.

Nothing could possibly go wrong.

I'll inject here that it's obvious he cared about this girl. Feel some compassion for him, if you can muster it. Nobody Feng Shuis their bedroom just to get laid.

The two of them walked into the cramped quarters of the fortune teller in high spirits. Both confident that the cards would make everything clear.

And they did.

Super clear.

It couldn't have been any worse for him.

He was not amused. "What the fuck is this?" he thundered at the woman behind the table. "Did you forget about our deal?" The look on his ex's face screamed "Deal?"

The woman smiled and said she'd taken his money and done his reading after he left.

"You what?!" he stammered. His ex was now smiling, thoroughly enjoying the show.

"Yes. You care about this girl. Deeply. More than you realize. I did you a favor."

"How so?" he asked, his thundering and stammering winding down.

"This girl is the kind of girl who sends dragonflies to visit suitors and jilted lovers alike."

His ex stopped smiling.

"Now," continued the fortune teller "If you'd like me to tell you both honestly if you belong together, it will be another $100."

They both looked at each other. He pulled out his wallet and forked it over. He and his ex both leaned forward expectantly.

The fortune teller shuffled the cards and then began to place them on the table.

ome is where the eart is

(my contribution to *The Shitlist Pure Slush Vol. 16*)

Orville Hanson didn't think it was that big of a deal. Euphoria Rivers, Quonsettville's Chief Librarian, disagreed. It should have been a minor issue, but over the years, it grew into something bigger.

And dumber.

It started with Orville, both big and dumb, and his former career choice. Like so many residents of this quiet Vermont community, he was retired. He spent his days evenly split between sitting at the local café telling tall tales about his former life as an Elvis impersonator and sitting quietly reading in the library. Now pushing seventy, he still sported big muttonchops and lived by the credo "Taking care of business."

Or, as he would often say, "Taking care hof business." But more on that later.

If you're getting the idea that he dwelled on his past, you would not be wrong, which rubbed some folks the wrong way. If you're wondering why he said "hof," you're obviously itching for this story to get going, which sort of rubs me the wrong way… but I'm going to suppress my righteous indignation and get to the point already. (You certainly wouldn't be nudging Dan Brown to get to the point already.)

Orville had a problem with the letter H. It began when was young and continued his entire life.

The problem? He refused to start a word that began with the letter H with the letter H. He would simply omit the letter. To balance the cosmic scales, he would start any word that began with the letter O with an H.

When introducing himself, he would say, "Horville. Horville Anson."

This annoyed a lot of people, including a boatload of Elvis fans over the years and, more relevant to the story, one Chief Librarian.

Luckily, there was little talking tolerated at the library but it occasionally would flare up when the two of them bumped into each other in town. Particularly when Orville was holding court at the café, the very same café that Euphoria frequented for lunch due to its close proximity to the library. Having traveled a lot more than most residents, he would spin endless yarns about his time in Vegas and the debauchery that transpired during his many cross-country tours.

"Hello, Horville," she would begin.

"The name is Horville," he would reply, sounding an awful lot like The King.

Everyone braced themselves for what was sure to follow.

"Are you telling everyone about the glory days of singing 'Eartbreak Otel?'" she would start in.

"Are you making fun of my speech impediment?" he would counter.

"It's not a speech impediment, Horville. It's a decision to misuse the English language," she would recounter. "A conscious decision."

"Since I was a kid?" he would thunder.

"According to you!" she would rethunder.

"Do you really think I enjoyed singing *'Ound Dog'* and *'Awaiian Sunset?'* It cost me gigs! I could ave been uge," he would say in a houtraged tone (crap, now he has me doing it) .

"Huge. You could have been huge, Orville."

There would typically be a pause while both parties debated continuing the exchange. Typically, they would decide to continue the exchange. Typically, people were happy they did as it usually got better after the opening salvos.

There would be personal attacks and nasty inferences made. In a small town, this passed for entertainment. But then, one fateful day, a light suddenly shone in Euphoria Rivers' eyes. She looked, unironically, euphoric.

"Orville… did you ever play in Horegon?" she inquired.

He nodded to the affirmative, pushing down his anger at her slight.

"Hoklahoma?"

Nod.

"Hohio?"

"What's your point, Mrs. Rivers?" he asked.

"When you played these places, did you sing *'Heartbreak Hotel'* and *'Hound Dog?'"*

"You know I did," he replied, wondering what she was getting at.

"But you sang them as *'Eartbreak Otel'* and *'Ound Dog'* correct?" "That is correct," he finally said.

"But you say things that begin with an O with an H, don't you?" she said and a small smile crept across her face. "You say things that begin with an O with an H when you're singing honstage in Horlando, correct?"

Orville, as big and dumb as advertised, still didn't know what she was driving at. Those around him had put the pieces together and began to shift in their seats uncomfortably.

Finally she came out with it. "Orville… otel and ound begin with an O. Thus you should pronounce them hotel and hound."

Orville Hanson mulled it over awhile with an I-never-thought-of-it-like-that expression then attempted to say either word. Unsuccessfully.

"Don't mess with my language," Euphoria finally stated, breaking the tension. Then she swiveled her hips, twitched her upper lip as Presley-esque as she could muster, and said, "Thank you. Thank you very much," before walking out the front door.

"Well… that was really mean," whispered Gary, owner of the café, to nobody in particular.

the trip

Time: 2025

"Houston, we have a problem."

Houston had been expecting this call from the moment they put the four men and four women on board the first manned spacecraft to Mars.

Greg, one of those four men, continued the broadcast. "Me and the fellas got to talking and…"

The man on the other end of the conversation cut him off with, "You figured out you'd all dated the same woman at one time or another back here on Earth."

"What?! You knew?"

"Of course we knew. We know everything about everyone on board. It's the primary reason we selected you and, furthermore, it was the primary reason the four of you volunteered in the first place."

There was a brief silence. Eventually, Mike, another of the four, asked, "Did it need to be the *same* woman? We were all flabbergasted when we finally realized we'd all been talking about the same girl." (The differences between being flabbergasted in zero gravity and on Earth, subtle as they might be, remain anyone's guess).

Greg, audibly irritated, said, "I realized it when Andy told us the last words she'd said to him. They were the last words she'd said to all of us." As if building a little suspense, he paused and then finished the thought in a higher, more feminine pitch. *"I'm doing this out of kindness."*

There were a few groans in the background that Houston couldn't assign. The man on Earth figured it was time to come clean.

"You see, gentlemen, the whole point of your trip is research. Figuring out not only if we can settle distant planets but who would be willing to make such journeys. Eventually, we're going to develop technology that allows us to travel at near-light speeds. Given special relativistic time dilation, as dictated by the second postulate of special relativity, it means we're going to be looking for volunteers who don't mind leaving behind everyone they know back on Earth. Forever. When they return, they'll all have been dead for maybe hundreds of years."

The vessel that was hurtling towards Mars with eight people as cargo got very quiet.

"What we needed for this first trip was men and women who needed closure. This woman, Jane, I believe her name is," - there were some grunts to the affirmative - "seems to have the unique capability of making men want to leave Earth behind after only a few months of being intimate with them."

More grunting and a barely audible, "you got that right."

"We're actually studying her as much as we are you. Her DNA might hold a clue to getting us an almost-unlimited supply of potential astronauts when the time comes. Arrange a blind date between her and a promising candidate, and he'll practically beg to sign up for a one-way trip."

It was now all on the table.

Greg spoke up. "What about the women on board?"

"His name was Tim."

On board the spacecraft, eight eyes sprung wide open and swung about the capsule wildly, belonging to four women who all sported a very distinct "you dated Tim too?" look on their faces.

The vessel that was hurtling towards Mars with eight people as cargo got very quiet again and a chill ran through the occupants. Not an easy task, given that the eight had spent the last few weeks traveling through an environments that sat at about minus 455 degrees Fahrenheit.

For a few long moments, it felt like minus 456.

Progress is like that.

Mother Jemima

A couple of things about me you probably don't know. I was adopted. Not a big deal; plenty of kids grow up that way. More significant though is that I'm white and I was adopted by a single black woman. Statistically speaking, this is highly unusual but when you're a kid, you don't really notice these things. You just notice the love.

If a guy can identify as a girl, why is it that I can't identify as half black? Just one of the issues I wrestled with as I entered my teenage years.

The other issue was that my mom always dressed like Aunt Jemima.

No exaggeration; she always dressed like the old Aunt Jemima logo with the apron and bandana and everything. The works. Her name was Nancy but her friends just called her "Auntie." Mine did not.

One day, I asked her why.

"You see, child, even if the bakers went to the trouble of cutting off the crust at the end of each loaf before they put it in the package, there would still be some people who wouldn't want the end pieces," she explained.

I didn't understand, so she tried again.

"I like to make whitey uncomfortable."

I was floored. "But mom," I replied "*I'm* whitey!"

I'll always remember the way she smiled ear to ear. "Yes, dear. Yes, you are." Her voice was so sweet, almost syrupy. "Let's say we're enjoying some Uncle Ben's white rice for dinner (coincidentally, Ben was the name of her ex-husband). The thing is, if a single grain somehow falls off a plate and finds its way to the floor, it will sit there unnoticed, sometimes for weeks or longer until it gets hard. Then one day, when you're walking around barefoot, you'll step on it and it'll hurt. You'll forget all about how delicious the rice was during the meal and just feel the pain."

Ben had left her for a white woman.

She leaned forward and scooped me up into one of her big hugs that I loved so much.

If a guy can identify as a girl, why can't I identify as half crazy?

Or should I say *only* half crazy?

Dear Stacy

Dear Stacy,

It's been awhile since we corresponded, so I thought I'd be the bigger person and write to you. I know we left on bad terms but my desire to drive a claw hammer into your head has passed, although I must say that when this desire was upon me, I would have hit you with the claw side of the hammer and with such force that I probably would have had to stand on your head to pull and wriggle the hammer free from your shattered cranium.

Not exactly the tone that I wanted to start this letter off with, but I know we both value honesty.

I still don't fully understand why you insist that Head & Shoulders, a shampoo claiming to help control dandruff, actually dries the scalp and causes dandruff but I'm crazy for believing that toothpaste causes cavities. It's the same logic… think about it.

But why I'm really writing is to apologize again for the whole *"Stacy's Mom"* incident. From the outset, I knew how uncomfortable you were with that song and it was unkind of me to sing it in front of your friends. You know how I get when I've had a few drinks and when they started laughing at my version of *"Stacy's Dog,"* it just egged me on.

What totally crossed the line was when I started singing *"Stacy's Dad."* I'm not even sure where I could have fit in the impromptu lyrics "Shooting my goo into his ear." I guess that's beside the point.

I'm sorry.

There. I said it.

And forget about the whole claw hammer stuff… you know how I get when I've had a few drinks.

So, any chance you want to go out and have a few drinks?

Let me know.

Yours sincerely,
Derrell

Dear Derrell

Dear Derrell,

Thank you for reaching out. I know it must have been hard for you. Also, sending it by mail was a nice touch as I've never gotten an actual letter before.

I would like to act offended by the violent tone of your opening paragraph but the truth is, the last night we were together, I watched you sleep and wondered how long it would take for a drill bit to penetrate your skull and then slide easily into your brain.

I guess it would depend on the size of the drill bit.

The main reason I've not contacted you is that after some of my friends explained to my father about your singing incident, things got a bit weird. He seemed genuinely flattered that you sang "Stacy's dad has got it going on" and, even more troublesome, he's started to work out again. I'm just glad they didn't get to the "goo" part. Maybe you shouldn't come by the house anymore.

Every one of my favorite songs has "You" in the title and I sort of feel you stole You from me. If that makes any sense. Your behavior was criminal but not in the way you'd think.

I want restitution.
How about we start with a drink?

Sincerely,
Stacy

Dear Reader

Clearly, the recent interactions between Stacy and Derrell were brilliant and could be part of a series of letters that continues from now until 2020.

But that's not how I roll.

Having said that, I just want to be clear that if I wanted to, I could have taken these two characters and made them beloved literary figures that your children's children would have read about.

Don't believe me?

Ok. The next letter would have been from Stacy's dad to Derrell. It would have been loaded with homosexual subtext (something about a half-shirt) and mentioned how the dad shared an affinity for power tool metaphors.

See? Right there, you're imagining what he would have said.

The next letter?

It would have come from Stacy's dog, although I would have wrestled with making the entire letter nothing but "woof woof woof woof" (funny, right?) or a treatise on how licking peanut butter off of private parts is a two-way street.

Either way... gold.

My point is, the possibilities were endless and with your warped imagination, you would have enjoyed every installment.

And yet, I chose to walk away.

Why?

Because it's not how I roll.

Sincerely,

Lance

Charlie Brown's high school reunion

Nothing takes the taste out of peanut butter quite like unrequited love.

-Charles M. Schulz

The first thing most people will wonder when they hear about Charlie Brown's high school reunion is whether Lucy brought a football.

From someone wishing to write about Charlie Brown's high school reunion, this is tremendously disappointing. There are so many other topics that would seem to be much more captivating.

An obvious one being: was Peppermint Patty a lesbian? No. After a few female relationships in college, she embraced men and was married with two children by the time of the reunion.

Marcie, however, came out her sophomore year of high school. She is now a massage therapist.

I realize that the football is a metaphor for a great many things, but none as interesting as the fact that Schroeder, the piano-playing prodigy, moved to New York upon graduation from high school and eventually got hooked on drugs. His whereabouts at the time of the reunion were unknown.

Certainly, that must trigger some powerful emotions in you. No? The tragic artist? Nothing?

I almost hate to mention this, but Franklin, the lone black kid amongst the old gang, died at the hands of police. Really shitty timing to bring that up, right? I'd prefer not to go into detail. Not really a *Peanuts* vibe.

On a brighter note, Linus teaches Mythology in Literature and the Arts at the local community college. He is also married. Not to Sally, though. Sally remained obsessed with him throughout high school and was later sent to a psychiatric facility until she got over it. Word was that Linus wouldn't leave his car and enter the gym at the reunion until someone had confirmed she was nowhere near the premises.

Although not technically part of their graduating class, I will mention that Sally went on to become a psychologist.

Pig Pen cleaned up his act and now works for the Department of Sanitation. I would say that the apple doesn't fall far from the tree, but when I thought about that quote and how it relates to a boy surrounded by dirt and filth through his entire childhood, it made my head hurt. What tree am I referring to? Even Sally with her PhD would be scratching her head.

Sometimes, asking questions causes more (good) grief than they're worth. Like asking if the football was just the manifestation of sexual tension between Charlie Brown and Lucy.

Snoopy is long dead. He did not father any litters so that wonderful dog DNA has been lost forever. Same with Woodstock. He flew into a car windshield and was later eaten by a cat.

And Charlie Brown?

Well, when he went to college, he changed his name to Chuck and started a band. While he never reached any level of notoriety, he did get to nail the little redheaded girl after she saw a show in the basement of a frat house during college.

He ended up getting into chartered accountancy after college and lives in a modest house not far from where he grew up. He was married for a few years but, it didn't work out between them, so they split. There were no children.

Lucy never married. She is an attorney and the terror of Florida's Second District Court of Appeal. Her hobbies include biking, cooking, and Krav Maga.

I know, I know. All you care about is whether or not she brought a football to the reunion. Why does it matter so much to you?

Of course she brought a fucking football to the reunion! And of course, after a few drinks, she asked Charlie Brown if he wanted to go out to the parking lot and give it a good kick.

That's the nature of women.

And of course, he said yes.

That's the nature of men.

And of course, she pulled it away and he went flying and landed on the asphalt and needed four stitches in the back of his still-disproportionately-large head to stop the bleeding.

That's the nature of sexual tension.

And when Charlie arrived home later that night, Lucy was waiting for him outside his house and they fucked like wild animals. When Chuck climaxed, he let loose a resounding "AAUGH!"

That's the nature of my imagination.

Yours too.

A whole stack of memories never equal one little hope.
-Charles M. Schulz

finite jest

Do you ever catch yourself watching TV?

One minute, you're totally absorbed in the show and the next, you're looking at a rectangular electronic device with images flashing across it. When you're in the moment, you're in the show. It's all-consuming. It's all there is.

And then, it's not. It's just a picture, no different than pictures on a wall.

And do you ever imagine what you look like watching TV? Like if someone was watching you from outside. Watching you watch TV.

Pull back even further. Sitting on the couch, but imagining yourself high above your neighborhood. You're a bird flying and soaring, looking down at it all. While you've been watching TV, nothing has stopped. The world is barreling on.

And then, you get sucked back into the program and you're totally lost in it again. The house disappears and the pictures on the wall disappear and you disappear.

I've had it happen when I'm watching a bad movie at the theater. I look around at all the people in the darkness. At the ceiling and at the bucket of popcorn in my lap. Wishing the movie was better so I could lose myself once more.

I used to travel a lot. The same thing would happen with the people I would meet. I'm there and they're there and then one or both of us aren't.

Wishing the conversation was better or they were better or I was better. Sometimes, we'd keep talking, but I was a bird looking down at the building. Sometimes, I could actually feel the wind on my face.

And which of these realities was the TV show and which was me on the couch? Sometimes, I couldn't tell.

Sometimes it was a show about birds.

the penis crisis revisited

If you're unfortunate enough to read my webpage on an ongoing basis, you'll know I've mentioned my feelings about the ridiculous number of nerve-endings in the male genitalia many times. An excessive amount. It was only after watching a film of an erotic nature that I noted that it seems females' nether regions are not lacking in receptors either.

What's the point?

Well, I guess originally, evolution wanted to make sure people were having a lot of sex due to the fact that the population was always hanging on by a thread due to starvation, volcanic eruptions, and people getting eaten by bears all the time. So, they loaded up the ol' sex organs with enough nerve-endings to choke a horse and the next thing you know, the planet is ass-deep in humans; i.e. it's about time evolution takes it down a few notches in the "feel-good" department.

I know personally I'm sick of spending half my time thinking about intercourse. Enough already! We have enough humans on the planet… we can retire the penis and replace it with something less "pleasure oriented."

I was just thinking the other day about how sexuality fucks up everything. Even the most benign interaction. A girl was recently at my house. Cute, but we're just friends. Petite. 115 lbs. soaking wet. Dry? Also 115 lbs. Never understood that expression, unless you're taking about a sheepdog or a gorilla. She asked if she could use the bathroom and I replied to the affirmative. She walked in and closed the door.

I heard the lock click. She locked the door.

A natural thing to do, right? We do it without thinking about, it right?

Perhaps, but…

We were the only ones in the house and she knew that I knew she was going into the bathroom. Nobody was going to accidentally walk in on her. The only logical thing to conclude is that she thought once her pants were down, I would barge right in and, unless the door was locked tightly, have my way with her caveman-style. I wouldn't want to but my nerve-engorged member would drive me to it.

How insulting that she would think that of me. I guess she might feel more comfortable if I installed one of those giant wooden barricades that slide down to bar the door, like the one they used to try to keep Kong out of the natives' abode with the big walls.

On the other hand, if I'd have watched her go into the bathroom and close the door and hadn't heard the lock click, I might have interpreted that as sign to follow her in and have my way with her caveman-style. You know why? Because of my nerve-engorged member!

If humanity found a way to replace my penis with a token that I insert into a female's baby-slot when I want to have a child, all of this could be avoided. We clearly have enough people; what would be the harm in switching out the equipment?

Honestly, I'd like a day without having to think about sex. A day? Who am I kidding? I'd like to go ten fucking minutes without thinking about it. I can't even type a sentence without slipping a fuck into it. And now I have to hope that my friend doesn't read this story because then she'll wonder what I mean by caveman-style.

Even I wonder what I mean by caveman-style. But I'll tell you this much: it's turning me on.

See what I mean?! That last sentence certainly didn't originate in my frontal lobe. It came from parts south.

Think of what I could accomplish if I didn't have a penis. Think what humanity could accomplish! We'd have had a man on the moon by 1920. But no, evolution is busy building massive football players with necks the size of my waist and penises that could choke a horse. And, no doubt, have.

Fucking football players.

Show me one NFL player that doesn't have less than seven illegitimate kids. Can't be done. Degenerates.

So what was I saying?

Oh yeah… too many nerve-endings in the penis.

Evolution, it's up to you. I've been a big supporter of yours since I was a kid, but it's time you stepped up and sorted out the whole nerve-endings-in-the-penis crisis. You have to take the responsibility of the penis out of my hands. And the literal penis out of my hands.

the clams finally came

Details concerning the origin of the phrase are fuzzy, but when Dave was a sophomore in high school, he began writing "The clams are coming" on every surface he came in contact with. Every desk, every bathroom stall, and every locker. And next to this, he would draw a single clam.

At first, anyway.

As the school year progressed, he would add a clam now and then. By Christmas break, there were four menacing-looking clams surrounding "The clams are coming." This gives you a rough idea of his artistic skills. Making a clam look menacing isn't an easy task.

Looking back on this episode of his life, he can honestly say that, to the best of his recollection, there were no sexual connotations or double entendres attached to the clams. This, despite the fact that he distinctly remembers a "bearded clam" being used as one of many (and by many, I mean over 40,000) euphemisms for the female genitalia. Ironically, his non-sexual clams often fought for space on desks, bathroom stalls, and lockers amidst a cornucopia of crudely drawn and fully aroused dicks.

The memories of the many manifestations of the male penis made him smile as he walked towards the back of his local mega-grocery store. He thought he'd treat himself to a couple of lobsters from the seafood section, despite the fact that he'd spent countless minutes over the years staring at the unfortunate occupants of the tank telling himself that if he lived closer to the ocean, there was no doubt in his mind that at some point, he would stage a daring midnight crustaceanal robbery and set them free. He was almost upon them when he saw the new tank.

And the new girl behind the tank.

The clam tank.

Mary, the new girl behind the new clam tank.

Just as he was remembering "The clams are coming." Just as you were about to forget that there is no such word as crustaceanal.

With only a few weeks left in his sophomore year, he had been drawing a veritable army of clams around his catchphrase. Nobody in his school knew who was drawing all these clams and even more uninteresting was that nobody cared. Not one person. No hysteria at all. Clams lurked in every corner and nobody even mentioned it in passing. He'd even started to spray-paint clams on overpasses and deserted storefront windows in the hopes of creating some sense of foreboding about a coming mollusk invasion but with zero luck.

He looked into the new clam tank. At this point, it shouldn't surprise anyone to learn that it contained clams. He certainly wasn't surprised, tipped off by the large sign announcing "Fresh Clams" that was perched on top of the it. A quick peek into the tank confirmed it. Sitting motionless at the bottom were a dozen clams.

"Can I help you?" inquired the new girl. She was cuter than most of the girls at the store.

The last day of his sophomore, year he realized that "The clams are coming" was played out. The clams were, in fact, not coming. They had never been coming and it was time to leave them in his past. To move on.

He never drew another clam.

By junior year, he was drawing dicks like every other guy.

"Sir?" the new girl persisted. Everything smelled fishy.

He looked back in the tank and saw that the clams were now in four perfect lines of three.

"I… uh……" he stammered and did a doubletake at the tank.

The older clams in the tank shot out their eggs and the more immature clams released their sperm. The water grew cloudy.

The clams had come.

Mary, the new girl behind the new tank, noticed this as well. It was clear she was disgusted.

"I wouldn't eat these if I were you," she said and made an unpleasant face.

Dave cleared his throat, straightened up to his full height, looked her directly in the eyes and asked, "Do you want to hear what I used to draw in high school?"

I dreamt a little dream of me

*"At the heart of quantum mechanics is a rule
that sometimes governs politicians or CEOs –
as long as no one is watching, anything goes."*
-Lawrence M. Krauss

I had a dream in which a mathematician came up with a unique solution to the over-crowding issue and I was one of a team of astronauts sent out to prove whether or not it would work.

I could provide you additional details, but by the end of this, your imagination will be taxed enough without trying to make you picture some nerdy mathematician in the first paragraph. I'll let you know when I want you to expend your finite energies.

The premise was simple- unless you want to look at the seventeen thousand pages of math that proved it was possible. Most of that math included squiggly lines that seemed like they were made up on the spot but were instead symbols used in quantum physics as routinely as the numbers zero through nine.

The simple premise?

That if astronauts were sent off into space on a rocket of unimaginable power (unimaginable until recently anyway) for a certain distance and then returned back home through a small fold in the space/time continuum, we would find everything as we left it… except for one small detail.

Every human, along with some hominids (great apes), would be gone. Or shifted or moved on or something. It wouldn't be Earth as if no humans had ever been there at all, overgrown with vegetation or run by cockroaches. Nope. It would be Earth just as we left it, just devoid of people. Every building and radio tower and ice cream truck would be sitting right there waiting for us.

Eventually, in my dream, we blasted off and went hurtling through space for the requisite amount of time until it was time to hang a U-turn, which we did. Soon afterwards, we fiddled with some knobs and slipped through a small tear in the fabric of reality, putting down landing gear back where we started.

I have dreamt many a crazy dream, but when I looked out the window as we went through the makeshift wormhole, it will always remain the most interesting image my mind has ever created. Really. I'm so happy with my brain. To try and describe it to you in any significant way would be doing it a disservice. Remember when I mentioned your finite energies? This might be a good time to expend a little.

But don't get discouraged if you don't come up with anything more than the usual garden-variety *Star Wars* hyperspace or *Star Trek* warp speed visuals. Try it again when you're asleep tonight and see if you don't do better.

Anyway, we touched down and soon, some of the crew were out of the vessel, walking around a completely deserted city.

It worked. It worked! Euphoria.

My shipmates were both ecstatic and terrified.

"What now?" they all seemed to be asking.

Finally, I got out and walked into the street only to find it full of people. I reported this to my associates and they came running back to see approximately a dozen people milling around me confused. Very confused.

In my headset, I heard the captain of the mission, a much brighter guy than me, asking me to come with all haste into a small convenience store just around the corner and I did exactly that.

I strode in to see him standing in the middle of the store and behind the counter there was a young man ringing up items for an old lady while two teenagers were in the back, opening a refrigerator to fish out some sodas.

"Oh shit," he said under his breath. "There was nobody in here until you walked in."

"What are you saying?" I asked.

"I'm saying get back to the ship and stay there before you repopulate the whole damn planet."

So I walked back to the ship, all the while seeing people popping into existence from who-knows-where. I wondered quickly if I could find my ex (does she have to be in every damn dream?).

Once back in the ship, I sat and listened to the other members of my team debate what to do with me. One of them suggested that it might be necessary to kill me.

The last thing I remember thinking before I woke up was that if I were in their place, I might have suggested the same thing.

"As far as the laws of mathematics refer to reality, they are not certain; and as far as they are certain, they do not refer to reality."

- Albert Einstein

Heaven

Craig has a problem. In a place where you're not supposed to have problems.

Let's get this out of the way right now… if you have consciousness, you have problems. Even in Heaven.

His problem? His second wife just passed away and is on her way up. He currently lives, very happily, with his first wife. His first love. His soulmate. His second wife? Not so much. She was better than living alone for the last years of his life. Barely.

But she shufflel'd off this mortall coile nonetheless, after a fairly pious life, which could make the next billion years or so seem like an eternity. (Please reread that last line to really let it sink in how absolutely gorgeous it is.)

How does he know she's on her way? You get updates when the people you know are about to die. It allows you make plans to greet them upon their arrival or figure out a good excuse why you don't want to hang out with them.

You know all the stories about how the departed can look down on you? All true. There's a viewing area with telescopes. What they don't tell you is that you're just as likely to catch your teenage grandson jerking off or taking a crap as you are seeing him graduate or walking a little old lady across the street.

You can sit all day and watch people on Earth go about their lives if you want. Heaven is a heaven for Peeping Toms. (Please appreciate this for the brilliant quote it is. You read it here first.)

Craig wanted to check in on his second wife's funeral and sure enough, the priest was going on about how much she was looking forward to spending her afterlife with him.

"Shit," was all he could say in response.

The idea that everyone gets along in Heaven is greatly overblown. Sure, when the Big Guy's around, everyone's on their best behavior, but once He is out of earshot, the usual arguments erupt and feathers fly.

Craig still hasn't broken it to his first wife that his second will be joining them soon. She was never a fan of *Three's Company* when she was alive; he fears she'll take the news about this new scenario poorly. The truth is, Craig doesn't even like the idea of having two wives at the same time. One is plenty. The Big Guy frowns on polygamy on Earth, there aren't a lot of fundamentalist Mormons running around topside, so he's not sure why He allows it Heaven. It's not like Craig didn't think his second wife belonged in Heaven- he would never want her shipped elsewhere- it's just that he's all set in the wife department.

Craig is in a real pickle.

You want more about Heaven? Details and such?

A bit hard to articulate, actually. Craig would probably tell you that it's a lot like Earth except for the clouds and wings and such. You eat if you like eating, but you don't have to poop. There isn't sex (the Big Guy is really hung up on that) but you can experience an almost orgasmic-like state just by being nice to someone else. People gather just to be nice to each other.

It gets awkward sometimes.

Speaking of awkward, in an hour, his second wife will be making her way through the pearly gates and Craig has to decide how to handle it.

Do you sleep in Heaven?

Nope. You're bright-eyed and bushy-tailed 24/7.

Do the days seem to drag a bit?

Not as much as you'd think. They have every board game ever made.

Are you forever the age that you died or are you the best version of yourself in perpetuity?

What do you think?

Are there retarded people in Heaven and, if so, do they stay retarded or does the Big Guy fix their chromosomal variants?

No fucking way I'm touching that one.

Are you able to avoid seeing people you don't want to see, even if they want to see you? What if they can't be truly happy without being with you but you can't be truly happy by being with them? Can two people exist in that same space and both get what they want out of Heaven?

"Craig!" he heard someone cry out lovingly behind him.

His second wife had gotten in early.

happy birthday, dear

He pulled some strings.

Some pretty big strings.

It was important that this year, his birthday gift to her didn't disappoint. He was so sick of seeing the crestfallen look that followed every unwrapping. No matter what thought or effort he put into it, he'd always manage to come up with something disappointing.

Not this year.

No sir.

This year he'd hit a home run. No more pottery courses or hours spent in a deprivation tank. No more Broadway plays or spelunking. No more jewelry, ant farms, dances lessons, or colon cleansings.

He'd arranged for his wife to spend time with God.

Not a religious retreat or visit to a church.

He'd arranged some alone-time for his wife with Big Man Himself.

Did I say he'd pulled some strings or what?

She was going to have a sit-down with the creator of the universe. Not just in His presence, but having thirty minutes of His undivided attention where she could ask any questions she liked. None of the "a thousand years is but a minute to Him" hocus pocus. Thirty full minutes.

The best part? He'd have to give her straight answers. No parables or metaphors. Just the facts.

As he filled out the gift card, he had to admit there was a little tremble in his hand. He realized that he was just about to deliver the best gift ever given. His wife was about to learn the secrets of time, space, and reality and who shot JFK if she wanted to know (or even who shot JR... she'd never watched *Dallas*).

He sat back and wondered what questions he would ask if given the same opportunity.

He sat further back- any further and he would have tipped over- and wondered if knowing the answers to some them might create more problems than the wisdom was worth. Was any human equipped to know this type of information?

And what cake should he get? He kept forgetting if his wife loved buttercream or hated it. He knew she had a strong opinion on the topic.

And what the hell was ganache? If he ever met God, that would certainly be one of his questions. He'd heard the term on the cooking shows he watched but never knew what exactly it was. His list would go something like: 1) Is the universe infinite or finite? 2) Why do we exist? 3) What the fuck is ganache? 4) Why do we have to die?

He tucked the gift card into a little envelope and smiled. He'd really done it this year. She was going to meet God himself. She always liked knowing something her friends didn't. They would be so jealous. This had to put him in her good books for awhile.

He picked up the phone and called the little bakery she liked and ordered a berry mascarpone layer cake to play it safe. Screw buttercream. A little more expensive than he would have liked, but he wanted the day to be perfect.

He couldn't wait for tomorrow.

rrrrrr rated

I think the hardest part of writing a pirate story is deciding what to name the pirates. When you Google "Most common pirate names," all you get is a list of famous pirates. Being that none of the pirates in the upcoming tale are particularly noteworthy, I was just looking for run-of-the-mill pirate names, not the big hitters.

It didn't help that they also listed famous privateers and buccaneers. While they were at it, they might as well have thrown in venture capitalists.

In the end, I chose Bartholomew, because it's very long and will give me the opportunity to whine about having to type it over and over again if I so choose, and Stede, after Stede Bonnet. Stede Bonnet was famous only because he was such an incompetent pirate. His story, however, is awesome and I strongly suggest you leave this story now and instead go read about him instead.

Still here?

Ok… but don't say I didn't warn you.

The young pirate put down the scrub brush for a moment to look up at the stars. Stede had been aboard the ship for two months and had yet to see any action outside of swabbing the deck. When he joined up, he had no idea there would be as much swabbing as there was. Feeling inquisitive, probably egged on by the cloudless sky and delightful breeze, he approached one of the older pirates to ask about this excessive need for swabbing.

Bartholomew looked a lot like Tony Robbins… if Tony Robbins had a lot of moles and sores. And liked to dress in pirate gear.

Bartholomew (holy shit, he has a lot of letters in his name! I'm tempted to just shorten it to Bart but that would show a complete lack of commitment on my part) looked Stede up and down before answering.

"You see that fella over there?" Bartholomew began and pointed a bony finger at another pirate who I will choose not to name. "He has a stone that we call a 'holystone.' He throws down sand and then rubs the stone over it to get rid of the splinters." He then looked down at their bare feet as if to answer why that was important.

"It also smooths away the tar that pops up from the between the planks," he continued. "Then you come along to wash off the sand and make things all dry again."

Stede was clearly impressed with this well-thought-out reply. He was also very impressed by the sheer number of warts a single face could hold without pulling the skin right off the skull.

After a pause, the older pirate asked Stede, "Not what you thought it would be like?"

"Not really," was his reply.

"Well, that's life, I suppose" said Bartholomew and Stede braced for what surely was going to be a long-winded allegory about sailing and destinations and storms and battles and calm seas and swabbing and death.

What he got was this:

"When I was your age, I slept twelve to fourteen hours a day. I was known as the laziest man in town. Sure, I held a job but you can be sure that the moment that the work day ended, I was headed back to bed."

Bartholomew looked at Stede and awaited the inevitable "Why was that?" but it never came. Instead, Stede seemed to be counting the number of visible lesions on Bartholomew. Having started his tale, Bartholomew ignored this social faux pas and continued.

"When I reached the age of thirty, I realized I'd slept enough and became a pirate. I've never needed to sleep a wink since."

"St. Nicholas of Myra!" thought Stede to himself "I have never seen so many scabs!"

"I speak the truth or let the captain have me walk the plank!" Bartholomew said sincerely. "If you come out here in the depths of night, you'll find me in this exact spot."

"I think that would be much better," Stede again thought to himself. "Your complexion leads to darkness being an ally."

"So what do you make of that, lad?" asked Bartholomew.

"Do you ever regret spending so much of your time on land, as a youth, asleep?" he was finally able to query.

After a long pause, Bartholomew looked him the eye and roared, "Shiver me timbers, you yellow-bellied swab, get back to work before I send ye to Davy Jones' locker!"

Stede turned and walked away. "Finally… some real pirate talk," he thought to himself and got his first erection at sea.

the butterfly

She is a butterfly.

I can't claim to be an expert when it comes to the memory of the average macrolepidopteran, in the order of Lepidoptera, but hers is pretty damn good.

She remembers being a caterpillar. She remembers the chrysalis. She remembers her metamorphosis.

She wants to do it again.

All of her butterfly friends tell her she can't. That being a butterfly is the end of the road. The finished product. "You've got wings and beautiful colors… what more do you want?" is a common reply to her seemingly-endless inquiries.

She doesn't believe she's complete. She wants to know what comes next. What's after the butterfly stage?

She keeps having dreams about being a bird. One night, it's a swan, the next, a cuckoo.

"That can't be it. I don't want to eat worms. Right now, I sip nectar from flowers. Worms are gross."

One night, she dreamt she was a pterodactyl. Soaring and terrifying. She eliminated that from the list of possible options.

She isn't content just being a butterfly. "So, you're telling me I have this long proboscis and it's not used in mating? What a waste."

She had a nightmare that she was human. In it, she was sitting on a toilet making beautiful origami animals out of toilet paper and then, when she was done with her bowel movement, used all of them to wipe her human ass.

So she went looking for a good spot to start her next transformation. Eventually she found a quiet out-of-the-way branch and began to create a silk button from which to hang. Family and friends visited her to explain that she was wasting her time. Perhaps even worse.

"Do you know how many insects would give their left mandible to be you?" they said.

"Do you know how vulnerable you will be hanging there defenseless? There are so many wasps around," they warned.

"What about that nice moth that fell in love with you? How can you leave him?" they implored.

Recreating the cremaster she had when she was a caterpillar was a bit tricky. Butterflies typically have little use for a hook-covered appendage (I worried that you didn't know what a cremaster was, but didn't want to embarrass you).

I can't claim to be an expert when it comes to how bright the average macrolepidopteran is, but she is not only smart but creative. It wasn't long before she had fashioned her cremaster.

Other butterflies stopped visiting her. It was hard for her to say why. Was it they couldn't bear to watch her fail?

Or was it they couldn't bear to watch her succeed?

Either way, the day fast approached when it would be time to create her chrysalis. The last time, in the simpler caterpillar days, she simply used her skin. This metamorphosis would require her giving up her wings. Leaving her hanging upside down naked with no idea what, if anything, would happen.

Quite a risk.

Then, on the day she was to commit to the endeavor, she was visited by the wisest butterfly in the garden (picture him in glasses, if it helps). He explained that within a caterpillar, there is a chemical that tells it when it's time to become a butterfly. There is simply no such chemical in a butterfly. What she was feeling, what she was doing, was wrong.

He looked at her and said "Don't you remember the first metamorphosis? How uncomfortable it was? The way your muscles and organs were digested to create your new parts? The way enzymes caused your cells to self-destruct?"

She just sighed. She remembered all too well.

"Nobody has ever tried this before. There's no way of knowing how this will end," he said flatly. "If I had to guess..." and then he just shook his butterfly head.

"I understand," she said, "It's just something I have to do."

He flew away.

She began to shed her wings.

Days later, a moth landed on the branch and there he stayed until he and the other butterflies and the entomologists and the poets all got their answer.

the road to Ithaca

There's a stretch of road between the middle of Pennsylvania and Ithaca, NY that seems oddly out of place. Hundreds and hundreds of miles where the road climbs and dips and on either side is a forest so dense that from above, I bet there isn't an inch of ground visible. If you were landing via parachute, you'd end up snagged in a tree no matter how adept you were with the controls.

That's the road I was hitchhiking on… so you can imagine my relief when a passing big rig acknowledged my extended thumb and pulled over to give me a ride.

If our nation's transportation system is a living, breathing organism, I was climbing up into its anus.

The cab smelled equally of a full-blown man-cave and a cave where all the large local carnivores went to take a dump.

The driver, Roger, extended his hand. I shook it and we were off.

I mentioned earlier the climbing and dipping road and I had no idea how it was to play a part in my ride. You see, while you couldn't really call the hills that we were driving through mountains, they weren't exactly hills either. There was no way these hills were just rolling. They were thrusting and jutting to the best of their ability. As such, they were playing havoc with the radio reception.

We couldn't finish a song before things would get so staticky that we were forced to change the station. I could tell this was beginning to wear on ol' Roger. Just as things were getting to a boiling point, there was a brief respite.

The commercial we were listening to was voiced by what sounded like a man who had moments earlier inhaled a balloon full of helium.

This delighted Roger.

"What the fuck?" he began. "They *chose* this guy to do the ad? This munchkin oompa loompa-sounding purple-skinned guy who lives in a tree and makes cookies?!" Forgive me if there were supposed to be a few commas in that last sentence but if you heard the way he said it, you'd agree that none were needed. Also forgive me if this little rant seemed a little hostile to little people but you can't always pick the trucker that offers you a ride.

Roger laughed the rest of the way through the commercial, no doubt wishing he knew a few more names for fictional little people.

When the ad was over, he was smiling and I breathed a sigh of relief. I had thought I was one interrupted-song away from being murdered.

A bell pealed.

Then again.

Not any bell. Oh no. A hell's bell.

Roger threw the truck into the passing lane and put the pedal to the floor as AC/DC blared out of the speakers. All was right with the world. If joy was a noise…

And then…

"Cause if good's on the left, Then I'm stickin' to the right"

(a little crackle… please…. noooooooooo)

And then, a lot of crackle.

Soon Angus and the boys were being drowned out by static and then, as if disproving a loving god, another radio station was joining in. A country and western song about heartache and alcohol, if I'm not mistaken.

I slowly looked over to see how Roger was taking it.

"There should be a law!" he thundered "Making it illegal to start *'Hell's Bells'* unless everyone in your listenership can hear the entire song without interruption!"

It appeared my grisly demise was back on.

"I agree," I offered up meekly, wondering if there was paper and pen available for me to jot down a few last goodbyes to family and friends. There wasn't.

Roger continued. "Make it punishable by lethal injection to have that song play and be interrupted by static! Drag out the staff of the station and shoot them like the dogs they are."

"How exactly would that work?"

That was me talking. I don't know why. My mouth said the words but I have no idea where the question came from.

"What?"

My mouth, fresh from its recent triumph, continued the line of inquiry. "How could a radio station guarantee that everyone listening would hear the song in its entirety without driving out of range?"

It seemed a perfectly legitimate question to ask anyone but Roger at that exact moment.

"It's simple math!" he replied and I thought for a moment that he'd leave it at that.

He didn't.

"The station would have to slowly boost signal strength. They'd have to assume that a car would start at the very edge of their signal, traveling at least seventy miles an hour, and then continue to increase the transmission power output for the five minutes and twelve seconds required for the entire song to be received by the car in question, i.e. about six miles further than its current broadcast boundary."

While my brain sat in awe of this quick thinking on the part of Roger, my mouth decided to spoil everything.

"If you assume," began its rebuttal, "that a radio station's advertising dollars are based on the number of people those ads reach and the number of people reached is based on the strength of its signal, it stands to reason that any decision-maker at that station is going to always have the transmitter set to its strongest setting. To think otherwise is foolish. And that's not even taking into account the Federal Broadcasting Commission sets strict guidelines about how strong a signal can be in order to stop stations sharing the same bandwidth from bleeding into each other's broadcasts."

My head hit the windshield hard. I had not anticipated the force with which Roger would apply his foot to the brakes. I literally lifted out of my seat and went headlong into the unforgiving glass.

"Get out," he said flatly.

I got out.

Angry at my mouth.

There's a stretch of road between the middle of Pennsylvania and Ithaca, NY that seems oddly out of place. Hundreds and hundreds of miles where the road climbs and dips and on either side is a forest so thick, it looks like an endless green carpet laid over the land like a blanket.

I got to know that road well as it was almost two hours until the next truck picked me up. My feet refused to speak to my mouth the entire time.

the pot calling the kettle annoying

People who call themselves innovators sure spend a lot of time innovating things that don't need improvement and not enough time looking at things that do.

I should know. I come from a long line of innovators. How this issue has escaped the notice of my lineage I don't know, but somebody needs to address it before I lose my mind.

Everyone knows that the tea kettle was a major breakthrough and I tip my cap to whomever came up with the idea of letting people know when the water has boiled with a whistle, but why hasn't anyone gone any further with it?

I was watching the end of a basketball game the other day and it was coming down to the final minutes. There was much drama and I heard the kettle starting to whistle in the kitchen, successfully letting me know that my water had boiled. I didn't want to miss any of the game, so I tried to ignore it.

And that's the problem with kettles. The whistling got louder and louder and louder and then I was standing in my living room screaming, "Shut the fuck up, water!"

Mt great-x8 grandfather Aldous Manion was an innovator (for those of you who don't recognize innovation, great-x8 means great great great great great great great great grandfather, thereby saving you from having to read the word great eight times... in theory). Why couldn't he have invented a kettle where the whistling stays at the same level?

Pretty awesome idea, right? Eventually, someone *will* invent this.

My great-x8 grandfather innovated Christmas. He was the first one to give his naughty child a lump of coal. It was a real breakthrough in child psychology at the time. It's funny how Christmas played such a large role in his life, innovation-wise, because he was killed the next year at a Christmas party. He and another man both showed up dressed as Santa. An argument ensued and he innovated the phrase, "Don't bring a knife to a gunfight."

He never got around to fixing my kettle issue, and nobody else seems to have either.

So, I was standing there as the whistling turned into anguished cries. "You're just water! You don't have feelings! You're not conscious," I implored as a player swished a basket to tie the game with only thirty seconds left.

"I realize," I bellowed, "that the transformation from liquid to gas might be uncomfortable but…" But I stopped because the kettle's screeching had reached an unbearable level. I was almost afraid to venture into the kitchen because I assumed by now, the kettle was bright red and the billowing steam was shooting up to the ceiling and melting the fan and covering the windows with perspiration.

Now, I'm certain that no squirrels will ever come visit me despite the squirrel-hole I innovated in my back door. It's like an opening you'd see for a cat or a dog… just much smaller. I got the idea while watching how cute the squirrels looked as I watched them out the back window one day. An hour later, after removing the door from its hinges and applying a little of the ol' saw action, I had a way for those little guys to come visit if they had the inclination.

Wasted innovation now that my kettle was refusing to pick a volume and stick with it. Nope. With every second that passed, the cacophony grew louder. Finally, in a fury at having to miss the end of the game, I ran into the kitchen and innovated/hurled the kettle into the backyard through the aforementioned back window.

Scared the living shit out of the squirrels.

The spirit of innovation is alive and well.

the thread

You see this other life, like a distance spot on the horizon, and you think if you could only change a few things, everything would be fine. Things would be better. This other life... this other path. This other possibility.

This other you.

A happier you.

There's a thread that runs through your whole life. Through everyone you ever met. Through every day and every laugh and every tear. It gets tangled and it strangles, but it never breaks. And it always leads you back to the person you're supposed to be with (not who you deserve... thankfully).

Those aren't heartstrings, my darling; it's just this single thread stretched between two hearts.

So, you pull it because you want something else. Something more. Something beautiful. And you think things might unravel but they don't. You hope things will change and you need them to change and you're terrified they will change... but they don't.

They can't.

There's just this thread heading off into the horizon, bringing you what you're supposed to get (not what you deserve... thankfully).

And millions and billions of miles away, an enormous ball of fire (enormous beyond our ability to comprehend), because of a reaction happening at the center of atoms (small beyond our ability to comprehend), sends a particle of light away from its burning heart and into the depths of darkness for a journey (long beyond our ability to comprehend) that will end up on our retina… and the thread becomes a web.

Our whole lives played out just to make sure we're there at that exact spot at that exact time to receive it.

That's the point, don't you see?

So you see this other life, like a sunrise, and you think if you could only change a few things, everything would be fine. Things would be better. This other life… this other path. This other possibility.

This other you.

A happier you.

And the thread becomes a web.

telescoping things out

Jim was weighing pros and cons while eating apple pie. In his head, apple pie was the logical choice for such endeavors. Nobody is going to come to any conclusions eating cherry.

Pumpkin? Are you serious? Pumpkin pie is something a Dan Brown character would eat as he wrestled with a decision and let me tell you, Dan Brown doesn't know shit about pies.

It was almost closing time so he invited the waitress to sit down and help him decide. He'd been coming to this diner for years, so it wasn't as if she was a total stranger. She'd helped him decide on many an entrée, so he trusted her judgment.

He unfolded the contract and invited her to read it.

"In a nutshell, what she's asking me is permission to occasionally watch me through a telescope," was how he began.

Eve's, the waitress's, eyes… I mean Eve's, Eve who is the waitress in this story's, eyes… Eve's eyes slowly made their way down the first page of the agreement (Fuck, that was an exhausting sentence. Hardly seems worth it now).

Jim continued with a little back-story to help her see the big picture. "I'm not sure if you know this or not, but I live in a high-rise over on 34th. She lives in a high-rise across the street. Our buildings face each other."

In retrospect, I should have used custard as an example of a pie you can't eat and reach any conclusions. Cherry, being a fruit and all, doesn't seem to be that different than apple. At least in the pie world. Dan Brown might not know shit about pies but I've never seen him have to admit a mistake halfway through one of his stories.

Eve looked up with a blank look and asked, "So what's the problem?"

"Good question," Jim answered earnestly. "On the face of it, it seems an innocent-enough transaction. All she asks is to occasionally check up on me. Take a quick peek into my life. As she explained it, it would be like being in the world's lowest-rated reality-TV show."

"An audience of one," added the waitress.

Wanting to give Eve both sides of the argument, Jim lobbied on behalf of the girl with the telescope. "She could have done it without even asking. I would have never known. I'm sure plenty of people in high-rises buy telescopes and check out the neighbors."

"Pervs," interrupted Eve.

"Some… sure. Others might just enjoy seeing what other people are up to. What they watch, when they eat, how late they stay up..."

"And some probably whack it every time a neighbor undresses," the waitress said, interrupting.

Jim laughed. "Ok, Eve, try to keep an open mind. She agreed never to record anything, never let anyone else look, and to never 'whack it' to me as I undress."

Now Eve laughed. A little too hard.

"What? I'm not whack-worthy?" Jim said, feigning hurt feelings.

"Girls don't whack it… that's all I was laughing about," she replied, still laughing.

"I bet you've whacked it before," he countered.

"A girl has to keep some secrets, Jim," she said in a failed attempt at being demure.

"Anyway, this girl seems on the up and up. She took the time and energy to find me. She just wants to watch people that are ok with being watched. Nothing more, nothing less." Jim placed his hands flat on the table, as if he'd just made his closing statement.

The real problem with introducing pies into a story is the reader's expectation that somehow they will be important later on. Like, Eve wants to open a bakery or her mother was killed by a runaway Sara Lee truck and I will somehow weave this into a brilliant ending where you'll gasp and clutch your chest and say, "It *was* a pecan pie after all!"

Nope.

This is a pie-less finale. I'm just telling you now so you don't get your hopes up.

Jim sat back in his booth and watched Eve sit back in hers. The truth was, as much as he wanted to have an opinion on the subject, he really didn't care if some faceless stranger watched him every now and then. He was ok being one of hundreds of people in a nondescript building in a big city. If he was in a reality show with an audience of one, so be it. Either way, what could it hurt?

He would let the waitress decide.

"So, what do you think?" he finally asked Eve after she finished reading the small print.

She folded her hands and looked him directly in the eye.

"I would have gone with the banana cream."

if you must work

"If you must work,
Work to leave some part of you on this earth."
-Keaton Henson (*You*)

Who can say what is worthwhile and what is folly? All I know is that once an idea takes hold, it creates a momentum of its own.

So it was for the Peoria Players, a theater troupe (of sorts) that did all of their productions exclusively for security cameras. Their final production took place in Peoria and some people claim it will continue on for years.

Right now, Gary Winters, co-founder of the Peoria Players, sits on death row, embroiled in a controversy that is attracting nationwide interest. He has requested a Big Mac, fries, and a coke for his last meal. The district attorney for Maricopa County, the family of Gavin Fitzsimmons (the other co-founder of the Peoria Players) and the McDonald's Corporation are fighting this request tooth and nail.

Why is this causing such an uproar?

I'd better begin at the beginning.

Gavin's desire to do something with his life. To be remembered for something. A grand and final gesture. A wonderful and terrible idea, the merits of which will be debated for years to come. The final production I mentioned earlier?

Gavin walked into a McDonalds dressed as Ronald McDonald and ordered food. Moments after receiving his food and before he could turn to sit down, Gary, dressed as the Hamburglar, walked in with a gun demanding Gavin's/Ronald's hamburgers. Everyone in the restaurant watched and laughed and pulled out their phones to capture the event.

Ronald refused to give Hamburglar his food so Hamburglar/Gary shot him in the chest. The loudness of the gun startled the onlookers and as Ronald crumpled to the ground, there were a few seconds of confusion as everyone was smiling awkwardly, wondering what they had just witnessed. When the blood began spreading from Ronald's body, the realization started to hit everyone. There were shocked looks on the children's faces, forgotten Happy Meals in hand.

Gary never broke character.

Gavin died on the floor of that McDonald's. As scripted.

Moments later, Officer Big Mac came in to hold the Hamburglar until police arrived. Eventually, Mayor McCheese also arrived but by that time, officials found the presence of these costumed characters unhelpful at the scene of a murder and roughly pushed them out of the building. Cameras from the local news station watched these characters mill around with the rest of the bystanders and the reporters were unclear what to say to the viewers about their presence in the crowd. Eventually, Gary's body was carried out, a sheet covering everything but his giant red shoes.

Throughout the trial, Gary stayed in character, despite the judge's admonitions that this blatant disrespect of the legal system would cost him his freedom and possibly his life. The media expressed outrage at the Peoria Players for continuing the farce after a man had died. Every day, more people turned up at the courthouse dressed up as the Hamburglar and zombie Ronald McDonald.

The judge would not allow Gary's sole character witness, Grimace, to testify in his costume so, with a final, defiant "Robble, Robble!" the defense rested. Outside, Grimace paced and robbled at the unfairness of it all.

After a few hours, a jury returned a guilty verdict. The judge, in her closing comments, said the following: "I don't know what to make of all this."

Outside, a scuffle ensued when a man dressed as the Burger King arrived, had to be saved from the hostile crowd, and was led away under police protection.

Almost a year later and after turning down every appeal presented to him by his defense, and with the day of his execution looming, Gavin requested his final meal: a Big Mac, fries, and a coke.

Eventually, he was granted this request, due in no small part to the influence of the entertainment industry. Celebrities, while unable to articulate why, felt a kinship to Gavin and loudly supported his right to a last request.

The day of his execution, all McDonald's in the US were closed for fear of copycat incidents. Outside of the facility that carried out the verdict, hundreds gathered and wept and lit candles and left piles of hamburgers as a memorial to the co-founder of the Peoria Players.

Calls for the arrest of the remaining Players eventually subsided.

There is talk of a big-screen adaption in the works.

Letter to Nabisco

To Whom It Might Concern At Nabisco,

Let me first start by commending whomever it was that first came up with the idea of Ritz Bits. I can't tell you how many hours I've wasted applying peanut butter to your Ritz crackers. The combination is delicious but it got tedious having to set up shop in front of the TV, individually spreading the peanut butter on each. When I saw that you were now offering tiny cracker sandwiches with the peanut butter already inside, I was overjoyed.

Let me also applaud you for calling the Ritz Bits and not Ritz Bitz. I am not a teenager nor do I work at a skate park.

Here, regrettably, is where this correspondence turns noticeably less enthusiastic.

First of all, after you open the box and try to get at the crackers, well… the bag has obviously been engineered in a way that nobody outside of power-lifters or sociopaths can open it. Pull it from any angle, apply any amount of force and the bag remains steadfastly sealed. I have no doubt whatsoever that elderly men and women have starved to death still clutching boxes of your product.

Once the Herculean task of opening the bag within the box has somehow been accomplished, the real disappointment sets in.

Having gone online to see the manufacturing process these Ritz Bits go through, let me tell you, I am impressed. The way the peanut butter is applied and then another little cracker carefully placed on top is truly a marvel of modern automation.

What your video does not show, nor could I find mention of it anywhere on your website (or have anyone from your surly Customer

Service Department explain to me), is what happens after the little crackers have been created and carefully placed in their box awaiting shipment.

I can only imagine the following scenario: once inside the box, you have some homicidal maniac specially trained in such things shake the living shit out of each and every box before it is given the Nabisco seal of approval. Up and down and side to side until they're absolutely confident that each and every cracker has been separated- peanut butter be damned- from one another, leaving nothing but a box of tiny crackers, no longer sandwiches by whatever definition you choose to use, where half of them have some peanut butter on them and half of them don't. After this is done, I imagine that you load these boxes onto a pallet and just before shipping, they are placed in some enormous machine that again shakes the living shit out of them all, just in case two heroic crackers were still somehow stayed attached to each other. I realize the chances of this are slim, but it just shows your commitment to fucking up my attempts at enjoying a fucking peanut butter cracker sandwich as I watch TV.

In short, I bought a box of your Ritz Bits cracker sandwiches based on the product highlighted on the front of the box and yet what I got was a box full of cocksucking fucking little cracker fuckers who weren't attached to fucking anything and, and despite defying the math, seemed like only a third of these ass-eating monkeyfuckers had any peanut fucking butter on them whatsoever.

It is my fondest hope that someone gets off of their ass at the plant and figures out why you insist on fucking your loyal customers in the ass so hard.

Sincerely,

Screaming at Snack Foods Near Philadelphia

Kinematics

In her case, it wasn't so much her restless heart that was a problem as was her rambunctious vagina. Which was ok because even when the sky was blue, she was always partly cloudy… although when she danced, it was like watching everything worth having in life.

Her mind worked in a very similar way as her vagina. You'd swear they were connected.

She wondered aloud, "How hard would it be to explain the concept of probability to an entity that existed at every point in time at once?" While I wrestled with understanding the question, she added, "It would keep interrupting with 'Things happen 100% of the time as they happened,' no doubt in that smug tone entities get when they live at every point in time at once."

Eager to jump in, I'd say, "And they'd know you were going to think they were smug and they'd say it anyway."

"They'd have to," she'd reply before falling silent again.

Forecast? Partly cloudy.

In a day and age where sex sells, you're no doubt waiting for me to dive further into her vagina but I'm going to have to disappoint. I weighed the odds of diving into the vagina of a girl who lived at a single point in time at once and realized that things that are never going to happen don't happen 100% of the time.

Restless hearts can be tricky things.

Labor Day (a story)

The business travelers on the flight thought it was some cosmic thank-you for their working on Labor Day. It's not often you see a celebrity, let alone in the cockpit on your flight. Apparently, doing research on an upcoming character he was to play in a big-budget movie.

If only the airline, which had been so eager to accommodate him and the studio, could have known exactly what the movie was about, they might not have been so enthusiastic.

Actually, they could have known- if they would have just asked.

The movie star was one of these method-acting types. If only the airline could have known what method acting was.

Actually, they probably did or they could have looked it up. The actor was quite famous and known for this approach to his craft.

Craft being another name for labor, and thus tying in perfectly with a Labor Day-themed story. If you don't think writing isn't labor, let me assure you that it is. Think you could write a better story involving Labor Day? I invite you to try.

Labor Day is dedicated to the social and economic achievements of the American worker. Just typing that elicits a yawn. But don't go yawning just yet. I'm about to end this bad boy with a metaphor that's going to rock you.

Not as much as a woman going through labor, I'll grant you that, but I had to include women going through labor to momentarily clear your mental palate before continuing. That sentence was a salted cracker between sips of wine.

And giving you an example of something that is typically used to cleanse palate was like a second cracker. Your palate is now doubly cleansed.

And you thought writing wasn't labor…

The business travelers on the flight thought it was some cosmic thank you for their working on Labor Day. It's not often you see a celebrity, let alone that he is in the cockpit on your flight. Apparently, doing research on an upcoming character he was to play in a big-budget movie.

If only the passengers could have known exactly what the movie he was researching was about, they might not have been so enthusiastic.

Here it is… the big reveal: the movie is about a pilot who intentionally crashes the plane he is flying.

I don't want to insult you, but I don't think you're taking the time to think through just how many moving parts there are in this story. A story set on Labor Day.

About laborers on a flight with another laborer at the controls who may or may not be wanting to bring the whole plane down.

The airplane is a metaphor and the pilots are a metaphor and the actor is a metaphor and the passengers are metaphors and crashing is a metaphor and life, yes even life, in this story, is a metaphor.

Maybe the only metaphor not being dragged into this tale is a woman giving birth.

Another salted cracker.

Method Acting was developed by the Russian theater practitioner Konstantin Stanislavski in the early 20th Century. When the Moscow Art Theater, under the direction of Stanislavsky, visited New York City on a tour in 1923, one of the people impressed with acting of the troupe was Lee Strasberg. When he started the Group Theater in 1931, he sought to recreate the kind of theatrical organization of the Moscow Art Theater, but one adapted to the cultural norms of the United States.

"The great secret… for moving the passions (in others) is to be moved ourselves" [using visions or experiences from life] "whereby the images of things absent are so represented to the mind that we seem to see them with our eyes, and to have them present before us."

-William Archer - *Masks or Faces*

But like everything else it touches, Hollywood eventually ruined method acting. Actors like Jared Leto, Daniel Day-Lewis, Philip Seymour Hoffman, Christian Bale, and Leonardo DiCaprio have spoken about how they lose themselves in roles and all have been accused of using "method acting" to both lend an air of legitimacy and significance to a performance no matter its quality and wrapping it up in a brand of identity politics that tries to make the art form resemble more traditional forms of male labor.

So, the airplane is a metaphor and the pilots are a metaphor and the passengers are metaphors and crashing is a metaphor and Russian ideas are metaphors and American ideas are metaphors and so is truth and acting and life itself, but in this story, triple-particularly because it's Labor Day, the actor is THE metaphor.

And like any good metaphor, he both crashes the plane and the flight lands without incident. The passengers die screaming and live to giddily tell their friends they saw a celebrity. Because the dream of the American worker today is both in tremendous peril and alive and well.

Because on June 28, 1894, President Grover Cleveland, whose statue still stands outside city hall in Buffalo, NY, signed a law making the first Monday in September of each year a national holiday in the hope that it would cause us all to write stories about labor and readstories about labor and remember why those fictitious yet all-too-real passengers sat on that plane in the first place.

Think you could write a better story involving Labor Day? I invite you to try.

2019/2020 (part 1)

It had been exactly a year since Lucky had packed up all his belongings and moved to Reno. Although he would hate to admit it, even to himself, he still thought about her every day.

Numerous times, he started to write her a letter only to realize the complexities associated with trying to tell your best friend about the girl who broke your heart when they were one and the same person.

So, he taught himself guitar instead.

In the spring, he'd taken a job that relocated him to Las Vegas.

"In a city of illusion, where change is what the city does, it's no wonder Las Vegas is the court of last resort, the last place to start over, to reinvent yourself in the same way that the city does, time after time. For some it works; for some it doesn't, but they keep coming and trying."

- *Neon Metropolis* by Hal Rothman

By summer, he could play most of the basic chords and had come to appreciate that gambling and hookers weren't in his wheelhouse.

"A little bit of this town goes a very long way."

-Hunter S. Thompson

The thing about a guitar is that it takes two hands working in concert. A partnership, although the roles of those two hands are completely different. The vast majority of people who take up the instrument, assuming that they are right-handed, can get the right hand stuff down pretty quickly. Up and down, hard and tender, the occasional attempts at picking an individual string. Throw in a little rhythm and you're all set to inflict songs around the campfire.

But the left hand…

The left hand reminds those that play that perhaps it's not a coincidence that the shape of the guitar and the shape of a woman are almost identical. Sometimes you play it and sometimes you don't, but you always embrace it.

The more he learned about the people who were considered outstanding at playing guitar, the more he noted a common thread that ran through all their lives.

> *"Behind every exquisite thing that existed,*
> *there was something tragic."*
>
> - from *The Picture of Dorian Gray* by Oscar Wild

The left hand is how the guitar talks. It's how it articulates what can't be said with words.

Sitting in his room, he could feel New Year's Eve coming.
"I miss you," he articulated to nobody.

He couldn't save her from what she wanted and she couldn't save him from what he needed.

He allowed himself to feel everything he'd bottled up. That all-too-familiar ache that gets pushed down. It was pushing back. He allowed himself to see through the lies he'd told himself for the past long year…that she was just another girl. That he would get over her.

2020 without her? "Please… no."

He knew the alternative would be even worse for them both. Sometimes, things just can't work out like the movies. There are no happy endings to be had. Sometimes, things are just fucked.

The tears wouldn't come, so *they* came instead. The Gods of Guitar. Surrounding him. Ghosts.

And with them… her. Translucent and shimmering. And still so damn pretty.

That's when Lucky found his left hand.

"You rest it against your gut, against your heart,
and when you strum it the vibrations go outwards for all to hear,
but the vibration also hits you on your body."

-Jason Mraz

10…9…8…7…6…5…4…3…2…1…

He played and hoped the vibrations would reach her as well.

passing thoughts

Everyone agrees that technology is making the world a smaller place… no wonder the seas are rising.

If you didn't know about wind, watching a tree sway would be creepy.

Typically, when I see someone dancing like nobody is watching, I want to point out to them that someone is watching.

I was trying to get a wakeup call but I must have hit the wrong button because instead, I got a rude awakening. At six a.m. the phone rang and someone said "First, your grandparents will go. Then, your parents will go. Then, you will go."

I was sitting on a plane, reading about deep sea fish when the well-dressed man next to me started flicking me with his tie. He kept at it, wiggling it at me until I finally fell for it and tried to grab it. His powerful jaws snapped shut, consuming me in one gulp. I woke up with a start, my knees hitting the tray table.

Nike has announced it will no longer produce Patriots apparel because the team name refers to people who support America.

Somebody had to explain to the word "it" that although it was making it into the title, it wasn't going to get capitalized.

Someone, one of those Good Samaritan types, approached me on the street and asked if I would donate money for homeless dogs. I said "Absolutely not. They'll just use it for drugs." I'm not wrong, you know. Pentobarbital is a drug.

Whenever I hear about activists, my first thought is always, "Get a fucking job."

Opinions are like assholes -and assholes are even worse.

Every story tells a story.

I watched a kid in a candy store try to articulate how he felt.

Hurricanes aren't all bad. You never see the beleaguered reporter standing at the end of a pier getting battered by a storm having to brush away flying insects. Too windy. So there's that.

Watch enough NBA post-game interviews and you realize you'd get more intelligent responses out of horses after they ran the Kentucky Derby.

It freaked her out when I told her I'd butt-dialed her. This was before cell phones. (Go on… picture it)

She was surprised to find him walking around inside her house naked. Even more surprised at the balloon tied around his penis. Happy birthday indeed.

Is everyone really ok with the fact that in ten years, high school American History will be teaching that the captain of the *Mayflower* was a transgender Muslim?

You know that scene in *Lion King* where Simba's dad says "Everything the light touches is our kingdom"? Imagine that scene if Simba had agoraphobia. Now imagine if it was Mufasa.

I was explaining to someone that I didn't like the chicken I'd eaten the previous evening. I called it unedible. I had started saying un before I knew what word, appetizing or appealing perhaps, was going to finish things off. I corrected myself immediately as I was unhappy with my choice of word. Or inhappy.

I'm old enough to remember when we called people "retarded." Then it was "mentally handicapped." Then it was "differently abled." Now it's "woke." I can't keep up.

Sam rode to the rescue. A happy story. Sam rode into the rescue. Not as happy for the dog. Sam rowed into the rescue. Equally unhappy but probably more interesting.

A new study released today by academics shows a direct connection between ________ and income inequality. (Fill in the blank with anything.)

I tried both Hot Yoga and Goat Yoga but neither really worked for me. Then I tried Hot Goat Yoga and fell in love. There's just something about the little guy collapsing and dying on my back that gets me in the zone.

I laughed when I saw a man with no shoes, until I saw a man with no feet. Hysterical.

Anyone who owns a bullhorn and is not part of law enforcement is probably an idiot.

Why didn't W get its own name instead of "double U?" To make matters worse, it's not even a "double U." It should be called a "double V."

You know how hard it must be for the folks at Spam to get emails delivered?

2019/2020 (part 2)

She'd been putting it off for a year now. By not returning the book, the door stayed open. There would have been finality in the act that she just wasn't ready for.

Until earlier that day, anyway.

She'd bought *Rilke on Love and Other Difficulties: Translations and Considerations,* a collection of poetry and stories by Rainer Maria Rilke, for an ex-boyfriend who had driven (been driven?) out of her life without even a goodbye. It sat on her dresser all year. A few of the men that had found their way into her bedroom over the course of those 364 days had flipped through it, made faces that reflected why they were so unworthy of being there, and closed it without comment.

She always noticed and felt a twinge in her chest, so she decided to paint one of his quotes above the door as equal parts litmus test to potential suitors and reminder to herself about what she deserved.

"I want to be with those who know secret things or else alone."

To most of the cavemen that entered afterwards, it might as well have said, "abandon all hope ye who enter here."

So that morning, she gathered up the book and receipt and headed to the bookstore. It was time to move on. On a whim, she wandered over to the Astrology and Divination section and picked up a paperback on tarot cards. She'd done this from time to time since college and, although it had started out as a goof, even the skeptic within her had to grudgingly admit that the cards had been oddly specific to whatever situation she was going through.

"Here goes nothing," she said to nobody and flipped the book open to a random page.

"The Queen of Wands reminds you to see through your creative visions and life purpose, even in the face of adversity and challenge. The Queen of Wands asks you to be bold and courageous in your undertakings and actions. The Queen of Wands also indicates that this is the perfect time to put yourself out there and meet new people. Finally, the Queen of Wands encourages you to get to know your shadow self – the lesser-known and sometimes darker side of who you really are."

There it was in black and white. Validation of how she viewed the world. Synchronicity in action.

She had always been right-brained, preferring art over math and passion over logic, and now, she stood in a bookstore holding evidence that there were more than cold hard facts at the reins of her reality.

Or so one would have thought.

But instead, she realized she was not as happy as she had been with him and decided her decision-making in the past had been skewed towards unrealistic expectations and daydreams.

(Only she would take a sign as a sign that there were no signs. Just in case you were wondering why her ex found her so spectacular. Honestly… she had me at the Rilke quote.)

She would make a resolution to try and be more linear in her thinking. Especially when it came to romance.

She drove home without returning the book.

Later that night, amidst the chaos and noise of the New Year's Eve party, she reflected back to where she had been a year ago. Both physically and emotionally. Wishing she was with her ex. Wondering where he was and if he was missing her.

The countdown to 2020 began. All around her, people were hugging and clinking glasses together. Toasts were being made.

10...9...8...7...6...5...4...3...2...1...

That's when she found her left brain.

She made a toast to him... and a promise to herself.

"I want to be with those who know secret things or else alone."

dream homes

There were two things that stopped Sam's ex-girlfriend Diane from maintaining the title and perhaps even graduating to a much-sought-after wife status.

The first was her toes. They were always in motion. She could spread them out until there was an unhealthy amount of light between them. They were like five pieces of kelp endlessly moving forward and back with the waves. At night, he could always hear them rustling under the sheets.

The second was the fact that every morning, she refused to have her bowel movement in the downstairs bathroom. She laughed when he would suggest it. The problem was that it sounded like some terrible wind instrument. A wind instrument that would never be asked to join an orchestra. Half bassoon and half wet moose mating call (Yes, while the noise itself sounded moist, it would take a moose that was itself wet to duplicate it. A dry moose would not suffice).

"For the love of all that is holy, can you please go downstairs to do that? It's the stuff of nightmares. You have to hear it, right? I implore you!" he would implore.

She would just giggle and say that everybody has to poop. What's worse, she would often come back to bed refreshed, feeling amorous.

"Are you kidding?" he would ask. "My downstairs is as smooth as a G.I. Joe after hearing that. A completely penis-free zone."

Which begs the question: are we really that uncomfortable with the human body that we can't make G.I. Joe anatomically correct? Would putting nipples on Barbie really put us on the road to ruin?

Given our technology, it would be (ironically enough) child's play to put a detector in G.I. Joe's penis that caused it to become erect when it was close to Barbie's tidy little vagina.

Playing house would become a lot more involved. Especially for Ken when G.I. Joe moved in next door to the "dream home."

There were three things that made the break-up tolerable for Diane.

The first was that she felt Sam could be petty at times.

He was also known to digress a lot.

And finally, her friend Joe was due to be discharged from the Army in a few weeks. She always felt that he had a thing for her.

So life rolls on.

suicide school

The hardest part is convincing some people that falling is enjoyable. They sometimes associate it with the feeling you get in your stomach on a rollercoaster when you slowly climb up and then plummet down.

That's an entirely different feeling. On a rollercoaster, and in most metaphors, you are being *pulled* down. It's not a free-fall.

Have you ever seen an unhappy person after they've leapt from a plane?

That's lesson one.

Falling is awesome.

The second requires an entirely different kind of leap. I would phrase it as a leap of "faith," but most of the time people associate that word with religion instead of science and in this case, gods have very little to do with it.

Physics, on the other hand?

Without getting into too much math, let me try to explain.

After a certain length of free-fall, once terminal velocity has been reached (a very ironic term, I'll grant you) -which for those of you who care, is 122 MPH- and it is certain beyond any doubt that conscious matter is going to return to an unconscious state upon reaching the ground, it slips out of what we understand as the space/time continuum.

In other words, it falls for as long as it likes.

Be it bridges or burning towers, people who apparently jump to their death spend anywhere from a few seconds to thousands of years falling and only hit the surface when they're good and ready. There are people who are still falling and will be long after their friends and family are gone.

We, as quantum observers, perceive it as instantaneous for some of the same reasons that time moves differently closer to a black hole.

The math will literally make you want to jump off a cliff.

Which is exactly what suicide school is all about. Making you want to jump off a cliff.

If the school had a mascot, it would be someone falling from a high place. It's really a win/win scenario. Either you grow to understand and trust the math and willingly jump off a cliff or the math is too difficult and the stresses of attending the class make you want to jump.

Either way… you're jumping.

The questions I get a lot are: "How did we find this out?" or "How do we know it works?"

My answer is, "That's why you have to take the class."

My next question is usually, "So, you really think you want some alone time?"

reading into things

Having taken the time and effort to switch sides of the table to avoid the beating sun, I was equally as put out by the rumbling in my stomach. When I buy a new book and the day is bright and warm and there are no distractions or obligations to take me away from the chance to lose myself in the aforementioned, the last thing I want to acknowledge is a rumbling stomach. Particularly because it was three in the afternoon and anything I ate would directly impact my enthusiasm for a healthy dinner. At two, I will happily grab some chips or crackers and at four, I am equally stoic in my ability to hold out until dinner, but at three, I sit in a land of shadows.

And sit I did, except on top of, or underneath or surrounded by, the shadows was in fact the chair I was perched on was one of the uncomfortable metal outdoor numbers that makes giving in to the demands of a rumbling stomach that much easier. Moments later, I returned to the table clutching a bag of cookies. Pepperidge Farms Verona Strawberry cookies, to be specific. Having prior experience with the bag, I knew of the upcoming difficulties I would be facing in getting it open. I gripped the sides of the bag with the same steely resolve you typically see when two enormous wrestlers meet each other in the center of the ring and bring down their hands onto each other with a thunderous slapping noise. Two cookies. That seemed a reasonable number to quiet my stomach without having any repercussions on dinner.

For those of you unfamiliar with Pepperidge Farms Verona Strawberry cookies, they are situated in three sleeves stacked on top of each other, each sleeve holding six cookies. I debated briefly whether to just extricate two cookies and then fold up the top of the bag again or fish out the entire sleeve and set it on the table in front of me. These decisions are the kind that take place in the smoky back rooms of your subconscious, where you hear the outcome announced but have no real insight into how the decision was arrived at.

Moments later, the sleeve was sitting on the table as I once again dove back into my book. Moments later, two cookies were making their way down my throat towards my stomach. A few more moments and my hand reached towards the sleeve of remaining cookies in front of me. It was like a horror movie made for cookies.

I had paid $24.95 for the book and only $3.89 for the cookies, so I was not prepared to divert too much of my attention to figure out why I seemed unwilling or unable to live up to my original limit of two cookies. It was simple economics and smoky back rooms and rumbling stomachs and the day was too nice to worry too much about such things. It wasn't until two more cookies had joined their comrades in my belly that I realized that while my eyes were engrossed on what was going on the pages before me, my hand was preoccupied with shoveling cookies into my mouth. The sleeve sat with only two cookies left in it, the wind taking the opportunity to blow it around the table. Action was required. I had to either finish off the two survivors or wrestle them back down into the bowels of the bag.

I did the former and then wrestled up another sleeve, placing the new paper into the old to give the entire structure more integrity as it faced the continued onslaught of a gentle breeze. I did this without thinking. I was six cookies in now, at a cost of 21.6 cents apiece, and suddenly, saw no end in sight to the cookie assault. The bag, now that only the bottom third of it contained cookies, began to dance on the table the same way those giant inflatable tube men dance outside car dealerships. Inside my head, delegates from the *Committee for a Healthier Dinner* stormed into various smoky back rooms with charts and graphs showing the importance of nutrition and how it is directly tied to appetite.

The book was a little slow getting moving and before I knew it, the sleeve on the table was empty and my hand was once again slithering down the neck of the bag and hauling up the last remaining cookies. I'm sure that Pepperidge Farms will be the first to tell you that Verona Strawberry cookies are not meant to be eaten a bag at a time. If that were the case, they would be laid out like Oreos. Dozens of them lying helplessly on their sides, waiting to be inhaled. Not so with the Veronas. There are tiers. Each tier more difficult than the last to get out of the bag. A bag scientifically designed to stop such gluttonous behavior. Even the opening of the bag is narrow to stop fat hands from getting at any of the cookies beyond the first six. 18 of these of these cookies should last a single consumer a few weeks. The only time you'd ever pull out all three sleeves would be at some social event. Eating all 18 simply wasn't done. These cookies were "artfully crafted." It said so right on the side of the bag.

A short time later, I wrapped the lone survivor in all three paper sleeves, it was almost ceremonial, and then retired into the house to await a dinner I no longer looked forward to.

Lance, the human Hot Pocket

For anyone who has ever had an MRI, this might be old news, but for those who have never had the pleasure of being slid into a tube and asked to remain motionless for an hour, I feel like some sort of analogy is in order… so here it is: now I know how a Hot Pocket feels.

You might think that this would have been a momentary feeling, but it wasn't. For an hour, I felt like a Hot Pocket.

Of course, thirty years ago, I would have said I felt like a Pop Tart being slid into a toaster but with the advances in microwave technology, I feel that the Hot Pocket analogy is even more spot on. I will forgo the obvious questions surrounding what flavor of Pop Tart I would have been, just like I'll avoid the question of what Hot Pocket meat would be lurking inside me. Those types of inquiries threaten to derail even the most stuffy story.

If, despite this warning, you feel the urge to shout out "Strawberry!" or "Brown Sugar Cinnamon!" I'll ask you to try and restrain yourself moving forward.

If you feel the urge to repeat the words "stuffy story" in your head a few times, I completely understand.

So, I was in the tube and with everything that I am- Enriched Flour (wheat Flour, Malted Barley Flour, Niacin, Iron, Thiamine Mononitrate, Riboflavin, Folic Acid), Water, Reduced Fat Mozzarella Cheese (pasteurized Part Skim Milk, Nonfat Milk, Modified Food Starch, Cultures, Salt, Vitamin A Palmitate, Enzymes), Pepperoni (pork, Beef, Salt, Water, Dextrose, Spices, Lactic Acid Starter Culture, Oleoresin Of Paprika, Garlic Powder, Sodium Nitrite, Bha, Bht, Citric Acid), Tomato Paste, Palm Oil, Margarine (palm Oil, Water, Soybean Oil, Sugar, Mono & Diglycerides, Soybean Lecithin, Potassium Sorbate And Citric

Acid [preservatives], Annatto And Turmeric Color, Vitamin A Palmitate), Whey, Soybean Oil, Fractionated Palm Oil, Modified Food Starch, Yeast, Dough Conditioner Blend (calcium Sulfate, Salt, Lcysteine Hydrochloride, Garlic Powder, Tricalcium Phosphate, Enzymes), Salt, Dried Garlic, Sugar, Spices, Dried Onions, Sodium Stearoyl Lactylate, Maltodextrin, Potassium Chloride, Citric Acid, Soy Flour, and Egg Whites- I wondered to myself, "Will I be delicious?"

It was a long hour, lying still while embracing my Hot Pocketness.

Eventually, I felt the little tray I was lying on begin to move and I realized I was leaving the safety of the MRI machine. My stomach tightened. What I waited for my whole life was about to happen. I was literally made for this moment. Was it fear or exhilaration I felt? About to be consumed. Transformed. I envisioned an enormous creature waiting for me to emerge so it could bite off my feet. I realized I would no longer feel them as it chewed, but I would still be fully aware of my fillings beginning to squirt out of my legs.

Am I delicious?

In the end, it doesn't really matter if I'm a Pop Tart, Hot Pocket, or human; life is finite. Everything we do is just a story and every story builds up to a conclusion. The best we can hope for is that we enjoy the ride and that story takes some interesting twists and turns before we stop being one thing and become another.

Did I find love?

Did I find meaning?

Was I delicious?

retaken

"Don't get me wrong; I loved Liam Neeson in *Taken*. I just feel the writers of the movie missed an opportunity to add a love interest.

Bryan Mills, Neeson's character in the movie, was single and spent the whole movie running around saving attractive females. Would it have killed him to ask someone out? Rescuing a girl from a drug-addled life of prostitution is a hell of an icebreaker. If you think *Pretty Women* stood the Romance genre on its ear, just imagine if *Taken 2* had focused on the ups and downs of dating a former sex worker instead of yet another all-too-predictable abduction.

Taken 3 could have been the one where we learn she was the only girl in the sex trafficking ring of her own volition. Apparently, the only thing she loved more than drugs was sex.

Poor ol' Bryan Mills. All the kung fu moves in the world can't save him from a broken heart.

His heart was 'taken'… get it?"

Alan the Clown leaned back in a high-back leather chair and waited to see the various reactions from the men and women seated with him at the long, expensive conference table.

Alan the Clown was dressed like everyone else at the table except he had on white face, a giant red smile, and a red nose. Everything about his face said clown, everything about his demeanor said not a clown.

Finally, someone spoke up. "I got two words for you Alan: Me and Too. Oh, and a third: Movement."

"So you're going to take another old successful movie and switch all the characters to female again? Lose another boatload of money to appease a bunch of pissed off women?" asked Alan flatly. "If that were the case, I wouldn't be here."

Alan knew deep down he was right.

When he was younger, he was a real clown. A proper one. Then finally he realized two things: 1) He liked to talk and 2) People prefer to hear the truth from clowns. Now he was the highest-priced clown in the country.

"So what's the pitch here, Alan?" asked one of the other movie industry drones at the table.

"No pitch. Just an observation," he replied.

Alan could have gone into politics. Given the current political climate, the country was practically begging for a clown, but the money was better in Hollywood.

"You can't keep churning out the same crap. You have to take a few risks. You have to make people think." When Alan was done talking, he looked around and saw a few heads starting to nod their approval.

The overweight man at the head of the table suddenly spoke up. "Challenge them!"

More heads started to nod.

"Even confuse them, right?" he continued.

"Yes!" someone young and weary-looking piped up enthusiastically.

"Wrong!" thundered the fat man, his chubby fists coming down loudly on the table. "Get that new guy out of here."

The young and weary-looking man jumped up and fled the room and didn't stop until he was back in Tulsa.

The man at the head of the table, who was head of the studio and a half a dozen other important interests, looked at Alan and snarled "Someone get that fucking clown out of here."

Alan smiled, slowly stood up, bowed deeply and exited the room.

"Now," said the man-who-would-be-fired-in-three-months-for-sexual-harassment-and-replaced-by-a-certain-clown, "Someone get me S. E. Hinton's agent. I want to discuss making *That Was Then, This Is Now* with the Mark character being rewritten as transgender."

"Brilliant," someone exclaimed.

"Not confusing at all," added someone else.

A woman in her early thirties thought about it for a few minutes and then retreated to the bathroom to splash water on her face. Her head swam for a good hour.

tom bo li de say de moi ya, yeah, jambo jumbo

Location: Suburbia. Time: The Present

As their kids stood quietly waiting for the school bus to arrive, two women stood a few yards away chatting.

"Did you hear about Alice and her plot to kill her husband?" asked Mrs. Anderson, a short lumpy woman with formerly-black hair (it was now mostly-black with grey roots).

"Kill her husband?!" exclaimed Mrs. Butler, a taller and less-lumpy gal whose physical attractiveness sat about ten years in the rearview mirror, the tone of her reply making it clear that she had not heard about the plot.

"She roped all of us in. We could have all been accomplices," said Mrs. A.

Mrs. B stiffened slightly as she digested the fact that up until that moment, she had considered herself as one of "All of us." Seeing her friend stiffening, Mrs. A quickly clarified her comment.

"You're not a member of the neighborhood Facebook group; that's what I meant."

Mrs. B unstiffened, so Mrs. A continued.

"Alice had sent out a message to everyone- everyone in the Facebook group that is- to flush their toilets at exactly 7:15 a.m." With that, a large smile crossed Mrs. A's face.

"What was that going to do?" inquired Mrs. B.

"You know how if you're in the shower and somebody flushes the toilet, it makes the water scalding hot for a few seconds?"

Mrs. B nodded.

"Alice thought the effects would be exponential. She wanted to cook her husband as he stood there in the shower."

It took a few moments for Mrs. B to process what she'd just heard. Her particular processing was a three-step process. First, she made sure that this scheme was in fact not grounded in reality. While her understanding of plumbing and septic systems might have not been on par with a trained professional, she quickly ran through the mechanics of such a plot to make sure that it wouldn't work. Once that was accomplished, she tried to internalize how anyone could actually believe that such a plan would actually work. She knew Alice and never suspected that the woman was a dumbass.

Finally, she wondered to herself what Alice would have said to police if her little plot had worked and her husband would have fallen out of the shower all red and boiled like a lobster. It would have been an open and shut case.

She wrapped up her processing by marveling how the ignorant can live right under our noses for years without anyone suspecting. Not so much a double life as a single dumb one.

"Can you believe that?" asked Mrs. A.

Mrs. B just smirked and shook her head.

"Turns out the police can't charge her with anything. Ignorance of the law might not be an acceptable excuse, but I guess ignorance of the laws of physics is."

The bus rumbled up and the children dutifully climbed aboard. Soon, they were rumbling off to try and learn something about math, history, physics, and septic systems.

The two women remained standing there.

After a long pause (news of an attempted murder is a hard act to follow), Mrs. B asked "Why did she want to kill him? Ben seems like a decent enough guy."

"Apparently," and with this, Mrs. A leaned in conspiratorially, "last weekend, they went to dinner with some of Alice's old friends and he embarrassed her."

"Goodness. What did he do?" asked Mrs. B.

"Details are a bit fuzzy, but apparently Ben had a few drinks and started to sing along with a song that came on in the background at the restaurant."

This was clearly not the answer Mrs. B expected. "What on earth could he have sung that made Alice want to murder him?"

"It's a bit of a long story, but Ben had seen some sort of *Behind the Music* program where Lionel Richie explained that in his song 'All Night Long,' he'd made up a bunch of lyrics to sound like they were African or something. Ben thought this was so amusing, he took the time to learn all of them."

Mrs. B's face was a mask. It was impossible to tell what was going on behind her eyes.

Mrs. A did not care, so she rambled on.

"To hear him tell it, he'd waited his whole life for the chance to show people that he knew these made-up words. He saw his moment to shine and took it. To hear her tell it, he sprang up, knocking over a number of drinks, and began hopping around belting out nonsense at the top of his lungs. Everyone at the Bonefish Grill was looking at him. She was mortified."

Finally Mrs. Butler spoke. "What was she thinking? She could have flushed away her whole future."

Mrs. Anderson caught the intended pun but did not laugh. She wondered if Mrs. B was even listening to her Lionel Richie story or was fumbling for a funny retort to Alice's assassination attempt the whole time.

As they began to walk back to their respective homes Mrs. B, still chuckling to herself about her flushed comment, said "Can you invite me to that Facebook group?"

"Will do," said Mrs. A with a wave.

a Valentine's Day story

Every Valentine's Day, I can't help but think about the one that I let get away.

How did I let her get away?

I'm so glad you asked.

She was always complaining that I never put any thought into my gifts so for Valentine's Day one year, I went the extra mile. At first, she thought it was just another necklace and made the face she always did when she was disappointed.

"Wait!" I exclaimed, lest she drove out of sight. "The charm has a special message for you."

She examined it closely.

"I don't see anything," she said, the disappointed face quickly gathering back on her face like so many storm clouds.

"It's a special charm," I began. "You have to hold it up to a wall and shine a light through it."

A ray of sunshine broke through on her face and she quickly walked over to the kitchen wall and fumbled on top of the fridge for the flashlight we kept there. There was a brief delay as she unsuccessfully scoured our battery basket to find the right size. She whirled and scowled at me- apparently, I had broken the sacred covenant about replacing batteries when using the last ones. She crashed around the house until she found what she needed in the TV remote. The way she removed them made it clear she would much rather have been removing them from a twitching Duracell Bunny.

"Like this?" she asked as she fumbled to get the light to shine through it at the correct angle.

"No. You're too close. Back up a bit."

Dutifully, she took a few steps back and resumed fumbling with the flashlight. Eventually, she started to see that there were in fact tiny letters making themselves apparent on the wall. She reminded me of Ralphie trying to decode the secret message from Little Orphan Annie in *A Christmas Story*. In retrospect, she should have been much more Gandalf from *Lord of the Rings* throwing the ring into the fire to see the secret message that was only revealed with fire.

"What are you on about, Manion?" I can hear you asking yourself.

Have a little faith in my cultural reference, would you?

She pulled the flashlight up and back and pulled the charm to the left and to the right; she could see a sentence forming. The suspense was building. Her hands trembled ever so slightly, making the words hard to read. Eventually, she took a long breath to calm down. She looked over to me and smiled.

She turned and looked at the wall and there they were. The heartfelt words that summed up that particular Valentine's Day.

I WANT TO BREAK UP.

So you can see why I get a bit sentimental every February 14th.

how I almost died 4 U

Disclaimer: Events as depicted in this story actually happened. The author does not recommend this type of behavior and cannot be held liable if you ever find yourself in the same situation and proceed to be a dumbass as he was. He is also going to ask a lot of your imagination in this one. Brace yourself.

Yesterday was just a day like any other. The sun was out and I was roaring down a back road with the radio blasting. It couldn't have been any more wholesome if I was eating apple pie as I drove. In retrospect, I would have been safer eating apple pie as I drove.

Disclaimer: The author is not suggesting you eat apple pie while driving.

That's the thing about muscle memory- a type of procedural memory that allows a certain motor task to be performed without conscious effort; you never know when it's going to kick in.

Disclaimer: The author had to look that up. While this poses no immediate threat to you, the reader, we certainly don't want you to think he's more intelligent than he is. Although, when you're done reading this, it's probably nothing to be concerned about.

And kick in it did.

Disclaimer: Disclaimers really fuck up the flow of a story. Sorry.

That's the thing about muscle memory, a type of procedural memory that allows a certain motor task to be performed without conscious effort, you never know when it's going to kick in.

And kick in it did.

For you to fully understand, I'd suggest you take a quick peek at the video for "I Would Die 4 U" by Prince. You know the little hand movements he and his bandmates are does while singing? I started doing them. I don't ever remember learning them, but there I was at 75 mph doing them. Over and over.

Not only that, but I started doing the entire dance.

Disclaimer: No, he didn't. Only a few parts... and not well.

After one particular shimmy, I realized I'd shimmied right over to the passenger seat. While the shimmy was all Prince, there must have been a little James Brown in it because while my right foot sat in front of me, my left foot was still on the gas pedal. And I don't remember how it got there. Fancy footwork was afoot. (Which is a hell of sentence.) All I know is that my left foot was going to take full advantage of the moment. The left foot never really gets a chance to accelerate/ shine, so it went for it.

It pushed the pedal down. Hard.

Do you think Price gave a shit? Hell no. He was just getting rolling. As was I.

Disclaimer: Sadly, Prince is dead, so therefore could not possibly have an opinion on the matter.

You might want to watch the video again to get an idea of the pointing, finger licking, and hair flipping that was going on in my car at 90 mph. I didn't realize that *Purple Rain* had made such an impression on me, but there it was. I actually ripped my shirt open. Buttons were lost in the transaction. If Apollonia herself had seen me drive by, she would have jumped in her car and given hot pursuit.

Disclaimer: No. No, she wouldn't have. That's a hard no.

For those of you who regularly visit my webpage, you might think this story is similar to one I told about what happened when I heard

"Feelin' Stronger Every Day" on the radio while driving. It's not. It's totally different.

   Disclaimer: No, it's not. It's almost identical.

   Disclaimer: Driving in a car with Mr. Manion is not advisable.

   Disclaimer: He's probably going to post the song lyrics now.

I'm not your lover
I'm not your friend
I am something that you'll never comprehend
You, I would die for you

-Prince

   Disclaimer: Told you.

the weirdo connection

Most of the time, I don't miss her.

And when I do, it rarely aches.

But sometimes it does.

Like the other day when I was driving.

And to be clear, this is not a sexual ache or a lonely ache.

I wish it was that.

The strange thing is that it's a strange ache.

An ache to share something that's weird.

And to be even clearer, I was in a car when it happened, but I wasn't actually driving.

I was sitting at a light.

Watching an old man walk back to his house with the mail.

What made it odd was that the man appeared ancient, well over five-hundred-years old.

And when I say I walk, I mean at a pace that was almost indistinguishable from standing.

I've never seen a living thing move so slowly.

And that's why I wanted her there with me.

Because only she would laugh at what I said aloud to nobody.

"That's probably yesterday's mail."

She would have instantly understood what I meant. Truly gotten it. We had that weird connection. That he had been on the way back from his mailbox for at least a day and a half and how funny that was. What a brilliant observation I had made. And she would have asked, with complete sincerity, if the man had perhaps seen the mailman return earlier that same day with additional mail and debated whether or not to turn back around to collect the new mail or continue his journey back to his house.

I heard her voice as she asked it.

And I laughed out loud.

And I missed her.

And ached.

Someday we'll find it
The Weirdo Connection
The lovers, the dreamers and me...

flush

There's a toilet at the Austin-Bergstrom International Airport that just might be the most interesting toilet in the world.

I'm guessing that on the off chance you're a plumber, your heart just skipped a beat.

I'm also guessing that if you're not a plumber, that your desire to keep reading just plummeted.

I'd better skip to the interesting part.

But not before pointing out that the most interesting part of the whole story isn't that it's true- it is- but how the toilet ended up being identified as interesting.

I'm guessing that on the off chance that you're a plumber, you don't really care either way and even as I speak, you're busy forwarding this to all of your plumbing friends. No offense, but not really the demographic I was going for.

But I'll take it.

Anyway, like all good true stories that are hard to believe, it started off as a whisper. Complaints kept trickling in to airport management that people were missing their flights. One person complained that the watch they bought at the airport store didn't work. Another blamed the ticketing agent. Still another blamed the food court for slipping him a "mickey."

Every story seemed to have a common theme: the passenger had plenty of time to catch their flight and had only slipped into the bathroom quickly before departure, only to arrive at the gate to find the plane long gone.

Most of the time, the next flight was already posted with the requisite number of people milling around.

I'm guessing that on the off chance you're a plumber, you're probably fidgeting and saying, "Get back to the toilet already!" You might even be regretting the decision to forward the story to all of your plumber friends before giving it a thorough vetting.

Relax. You and your pipe-fitting brethren are in good hands.

Eventually, an intrepid custodian was brought into the meeting to discuss the mysterious phenomena. What had been determined up to that point was that each of these passengers had gone into the same bathroom just before missing their flight and each of them had subsequently showed up approximately two hours late for their flight.

It defied reason. It defied logic. It defied another word for logic that would cement my unique writing style in your mind.

Eventually, the intrepid custodian was sent to examine each stall to make sure there was no funny business going on. He returned to announce that there was nothing unusual to report... to an empty conference room!

"Where did everyone go?" asked the intrepid custodian to himself. Then he looked at his watch. It was two hours later than he expected. The other attendees had long since left for the day.

The next morning, the custodian hastily gathered everyone back together to let them know what had occurred. They showed various degrees of disbelief, so he hastily herded them to the bathroom to see if he could duplicate the previous day's efforts.

He went into the first stall, closed the door, and flushed.

Nothing happened.

He went into the second stall, closed the door, and flushed.

Nothing happened.

He went into the third stall, closed the door, and flushed.

Nothing happened… or so they thought until one of them glanced down at their watch.

Two hours had passed.

I'm guessing that on the off chance you're a plumber, you're thinking this might be the best short story you've ever read. It has everything. Suspense. Intrigue. Plumbing. "Everyone at Local 690 has got to read this!"

"How did it affect us on the outside of the stall when it didn't affect the other people in the bathroom before?" asked one of the stunned occupants of the men's room.

"Are you familiar with the observer effect? Bell's Theorem? The idea that by simply observing a situation that you can affect the measured result?" inquired one of the airport's brighter individuals.

"No," replied the custodian… to nobody's surprise.

"Gentlemen, we seem to have found the toilet that time forgot," suggested another one of the bespectacled bathroom-inhabitants.

"That comment wasn't very helpful, Dan" said one of the airport's brighter individuals.

The group mulled over the situation for awhile.

"If this becomes common knowledge, it could have negative repercussions on a global scale," one of the airport's brighter individuals finally offered up.

"How so?" asked the custodian.

"Imagine a pilot finding out about this bathroom, being aware of it, and somehow being transported two hours into the future… in the middle of a one-hour flight."

Everyone in the bathroom drew in a deep breath and nodded respectfully.

Why do I keep referring to the custodian as intrepid? Because this is when he leapt into action and removed the door to the stall. He casually walked in, gave the toilet a flush, and nothing happened.

I'm guessing that on the off chance you're a plumber, then you're applauding his intrepidness.

Everyone went back to work.

So if you ever find yourself at the Austin-Bergstrom International Airport, you might want to duck into the men's room and take a look at the stall without a door.

The most interesting toilet in the world.

aaaaarrrmageddon

"Medical professionals across the globe are scrambling to understand what police are calling 'Sudden Pirate Syndrome.' What causes the unusual symptoms remains a mystery, but those afflicted experience a sudden onset of what can only be described as violent buccaneer behavior, complete with swashbuckling the shit out of anyone nearby.

Over thirty people have already been killed by SPS sufferers and the body count continues to climb.

The last attack was captured on security cameras inside a posh midtown restaurant. As you can see, the middle-aged woman circled in red enters the eatery looking and acting quite normal. She steps out of frame for only a few moments to sit down with friends when suddenly, she begins wielding a scimitar and cutting down any who oppose her.

We now go live to our reporter Sarah Johnson standing outside the restaurant.

Sarah, can you describe the mood there?"

"Absolutely. Everyone is shocked and saddened by this most recent attack."

"I can imagine. What I'm particularly interested in is where this woman got the pirate outfit."

"Excuse me?"

"Well, Sarah, when the woman enters the restaurant, she is wearing a blue pantsuit. She is led to a table off-camera and moments later, she returns to frame but she is not only wielding a scimitar, but she is dressed as a pirate."

"What do you mean?"

"I mean she has on a large pirate hat emblazoned with a skull and crossbones, an eyepatch, and appears to be wearing a long jacket and bloomers. Where did she get them from? How was she able to change into this outfit so quickly before starting her savage attack on fellow customers?"

"I'm not really sure. Would you like me to interview any of the eye witnesses? I'm sure they will describe her a quiet woman and be at a loss as to what made her commit this heinous crime."

"No. No friends or acquaintances. Not unless they can explain how a middle-aged woman who goes on a killing spree suddenly has access to pirate garb."

"Listen, this was just supposed to be a funny little story and the addition of the eye patch is essential in making sure the viewing audience associates the violent behavior with pirates."

"Sounds like lazy writing to me."

"Be that as it may, if you dissect every attempt at levity by asking questions that are, of course, impossible to answer, you're going to kill the humor. Perhaps you could argue that by adding the overcoat and bloomers, the writer pushed it too far but, in his defense, he did decide against the peg leg and parrot on her shoulder."

"So, we're supposed to find it more believable just because there wasn't a parrot involved?"

"Yes. Yes, you are. It's funny. Normal people suddenly turning into pirates."

"If you say so, Sarah."

"I do. This is Sarah Johnson, signing off from yet another bizarre 'Sudden Pirate Syndrome' incident."

the Emperor's new words

raise /rāz/ *verb lift or move to a higher position or level*

raze /rāz/ *verb completely destroy*

I'm calling bullshit on the second word.

There's no way it was intended to mean both. It's so obvious that somebody in a position of authority somehow flubbed saying "raise" in the right context and instead of admitting he fucked up, he probably stood there, fumbling around and finally spit out "I meant… razed…with a *z*. To tear down." No doubt, everyone who heard his original screwup glared at him and thought to themselves, "Just admit it, dude," but as this individual had the power to lop off their heads if they disagreed or embarrassed him, everyone had to keep their mouths shut and accept it.

The birth of a new word.

What's worse, I guarantee you that this same prick went around saying "razed" every chance he could from then on just to make sure that people started to use the word. Galloping around and forcing it into every conversation, everyone within earshot knowing deep down that the guy was an asshat, but also knowing that if they piped up, their next barn raising would end up a barn razing.

The irony in the meaning of the words is painful. The perfect metaphor. It makes you want to jump back in time and raze a toast to this moron. The mug smashing into his dumb, fat, smug face.

Oh, he was overweight alright. You can wager on that.

Thank goodness that words and their meaning are no longer under assault from people in positions of authority these days, right?

a chance meeting with Adolf

I sat down at the bar next to a guy who looked vaguely familiar, but I couldn't quite place the face. After ordering a beer, I introduced myself and asked him if we'd ever met.

"Nope. But I get that a lot," he said in a thick German accent.

"I'm Lance," I said, extending a hand.

"Adolf," he replied.

"Wow... that's a name you don't hear much these days."

He laughed and said "Yeah, that Hitler fella ruined it, right?" Except the last word came out as Reich.

I suddenly realized where I knew the guy from. He looked just like Adolf Hitler, except without the mustache and sporting a short-sleeved shirt and khakis instead of the epochal field grey uniform of the German army.

"You know..." I said as I struggled to find the right way to say it, "you bear an uncanny resemblance to Hitler. If you had the mustache." I didn't want to insult him, but the closer I looked, the more it appeared he was a dead ringer for the man.

"I get that a lot," he said. After taking another swig of his beer, he asked me "Do you want to know a secret?"

Always game for a good secret, I smiled and nodded my head in the affirmative.

"I *am* Adolph Hitler. Not an ancestor or a wannabe, but the real McCoy. Der echte artikel. The *actual* Adolf Hitler. I realize that would make me 131 years old, but I have another secret that explains it."

Instantly, the conversation got awkward. I enjoy talking to a mentally deranged person as much as the next guy, particularly after a few beers, but not being much of a fan of Hitler's work, I started to feel uncomfortable.

"Let me ask you a question before I tell you what that other secret is," Adolf continued. "If you had a time machine, what would be the first thing you'd do?" A small smile crept across his face.

"Well, let me see…" I began. "Probably go back in time and kill you."

"Bingo," he said and took a long swig of his beer.

Hearing someone who thought he was Adolf Hitler say the word "bingo" will forever haunt me.

I stood up to leave. "Listen, Adolf, it's been fun and all, but I got somewhere else to be."

He put his hand on my shoulder and pleaded with me to hear him out. So I did.

"Have you ever seen the movie *Back to the Future* with Michael J. Fox?"

An odd start if he was looking to clear things up.

"Of course," I replied. "Everyone has."

"How come nobody ever asked Dr. Emmet Brown and Marty McFly why they didn't go back in time and kill me?" He looked at me as if I should be completely flummoxed by the question.

"Maybe because it was a comedy…?" I offered up with no hint of flummoxedness.

"My point is, everyone's first thought when they get a time machine is coming back and killing me. Flattering, if you think about it. To be *the* guy everybody wants to go back and kill. Number one. Nummer eins.

The GOAT bad guy. The question you have to ask yourself is, 'Do you really think nobody tried?'"

He finished his beer and waved the bartender over to get another while I wrestled with this concept. Eventually, I shrugged my shoulders to let him know I was stumped.

"Here's the thing," he said with a conspiratorial wink, "they did. Three of them over the years. The thing they never appreciate is how hard it is to actually kill somebody. Two of them chickened out because they came back when I was still young and they just couldn't bring themselves to pull the trigger. I guess I was pretty adorable as a tyke. Fotzen. The third tried his best, but as a scientist, his assassination skills were pretty poor. By the time I was Chancellor of Germany, I had three time machines in my possession."

"I have to admit, that's quite a story," was all I could get out.

"Every word of it's true. Unlike the *Back to the Future* movie though, there wasn't a dial where I could set any date I liked and go there. I could only figure out how to return to the date it had come from. Which, and you want to talk crazy, was October 15, 2015. The same date as in the movie." He paused and then seemed to launch into his best Christopher Lloyd impression. "'It could mean that that point in time inherently contains some sort of cosmic significance. Almost as if it were the temporal junction point for the entire space-time continuum. On the other hand, it could just be an amazing coincidence.'" He sat back beaming. "That's a quote from the movie. Dass Lloyd ein pip ist."

It took a few minutes for everything to sink in. You don't know the meaning of the word disheveled until you've witnessed the leader of the Third Reich do his Doc Brown impression. "So you're saying you've been here in America for almost five years now?"

"Ja. One minute I'm sitting in my Fuhrerbunker with the Allies closing in and the next, I'm sitting in a secret laboratory in Columbus, Ohio. Really strange, ja?"

"So, why are you telling me this?" I felt compelled to ask.

"Why not? Nobody would ever believe you even if you went to the authorities and, to be quite honest with you, what's the fun of being Adolf Hitler in 2020 if you can't tell someone?"

We sat quietly for a few minutes. "Disappointed I don't have horns or breathe fire?" he asked.

I thought it over and said, "What is it they say about the banality of evil?"

"Touché, Lance."

For a few weird seconds, I realized I actually believed he was Adolf Hitler and suddenly understood what he'd been saying about how difficult it is to bring yourself to kill someone.

He could tell I was wrestling with this unusual predicament. He sighed, said "Take your time," and turned his attention to the television above the bar showing *SportsCenter*.

"Can you believe Tom Brady went to the Buccaneers? Who saw that coming? Und sie nennen sich Patrioten" said Adolf.

"Yeah… unbelievable," I finally replied.

"I wonder if Robert Kraft has any regrets," he said almost to himself.

"Don't we all?" is all I could say.

A few hours later, I left the bar without killing Adolf Hitler.

guy on a plane

As I sat down, he was already talking to his cup. He was visibly annoyed. I had the aisle seat; he had the window.

"Listen, ice, I appreciate you cooling down my beverage and all but quit bumping my teeth every time I try and take a drink."

He saw I was taking in his conversation (I was going to say "drinking in his conversation" but that seemed too droll), so he quickly switched gears and extended his hand. "Hi, I'm Brian. Where you from?"

I gave him my name and the city I lived in and hoped our little chat would end there.

It did not.

Over the course of the next four hours and forty minutes, I got to know far more about Brian than any stranger should ever have to endure. As we took off, he told me the story about how he had this big tree outside the house he grew up in and how special that tree was to him until his first plane ride where he saw millions of trees from above and how they all looked the same and he could never look at his boyhood tree the same way. It could still have the tire swing and the big branches for climbing but he knew deep down that from 10,000 feet in the air, it looked like all the other green circles.

I suggested the same could be said about women, but he'd already moved on to the next topic.

Which was pain.

He told me that one time, he hit his head so hard that instead of seeing a bright light, he actually visualized the pain as purple and black. I wondered what that meant and asked him for more information.

"It was like these black silhouettes of Valkyries riding down from a swirling purple sky. It was more like an apocalyptic hallucination than a head injury."

For a fleeting moment, I found him slightly fascinating but without skipping a beat, he immediately started talking about how women should always wear bras.

The impetus for this new line of thought? A woman was leaning over her seat a few rows in front of us and you could clearly see her breasts. (I feel I should be completely honest and tell you the first time I typed "breasts," I typed "greats." That has to mean something. Something pretty simple actually.) I turned my head instantly, embarrassed, hoping she wouldn't look up and notice me staring at her rack. Brian, on the other hand, stared right at them, the whole time extolling the virtues of modesty in this decadent age of exhibitionism.

When we finally arrived at our gate, I practically ran down the aisle to be free of him. It wasn't until I was waiting to step onto the crowded shuttle heading for the main terminal that I realized Brian was still with me. We boarded the bus with some minor difficulty as the people standing in the middle were not too gung-ho about being pushed together to allow other passengers to board.

Brian chirped in "White people aren't comfortable cramming together like Asians. Asians would have twice as many people on this bus without batting an eyelash. People of European descent don't like to cram."

I would like to say that I found this comment somehow racist, but I was too worried about using the term "gung-ho" when I knew there was a sentence involving Asians coming right up. People who live in glass houses shouldn't cram in too many Asians I guess.

I had no reply for that and we spent the remainder of the ride in silence.

Eventually, I made for the taxi stand. He left for parts unknown.

(All of the above conversations actually happened and were in no way embellished for your reading pleasure.)

Also, all of the above is what I imagine the guy in the aisle was thinking about what I was saying. Except the parts in parenthesis, that's what I imagine he would be thinking I would be thinking if I were writing it down.

the butter quote

Butter is almost impossible to get off of you.
No matter how many times you wipe,
there is still a film left behind.
It's like, if it gets on you, ironically enough, you're toast.

-Lance Manion

I know. Brilliant.

"How does he do it?" you must ask yourself from time to time. The endless flood of brilliant quotes and observations. "Where does it all come from, and why can't I come up with this stuff?"

Beware what you ask for.

In order to answer your questions, allow me to give you a behind-the-scenes look at my creative process. A step-by-step recap of how a brilliant quote is created. One minute it doesn't exist; the next, it's pulled from the abyss into being.

It should serve as a warning the next time you wish your mind worked like mine.

Actually, just this preamble should be enough… but I said I'd share, so share I will.

Imagine a kitchen in Anytown, USA. In that kitchen is a man doing dishes. A rugged man. A handsome man.

Ok, maybe not entirely handsome, but from the right angle… not entirely unhandsome. Either way, it doesn't matter. What matters is that the meal that proceeded the dishwashing endeavor included corn on the cob. And that corn on the cob included butter. Lots of butter.

Butter that ended up on those very dishes. Butter that ended up on the hands of the rugged and not entirely unhandsome man.

He tried to wash it off. It didn't wash off. Butter is funny like that. If you think stubborn foods are funny.

The rugged man did not.

In case you're wondering, I am the rugged man. I just wanted to make sure you were clear on that. I could see a scenario where you are totally lost. "I thought he was going to share a personal experience and here he is talking about a rugged man," and then I can hear you asking yourself, "do rugged men do dishes?"

Of course they do! Honestly, I didn't even see that question coming. I thought I had an enlightened readership and yet, you come out with something like that.

I'm prepared to forgive you, though. Just as you forgive me when my stories ramble a bit. Or a lot.

How else would rugged men's dishes get clean? Do you assume that rugged men have rugged dishes? And by rugged, I mean covered in mold and stuck-on food particles.

"Holy crap!" I/rugged man exclaimed. "I can't get this shit off of my hands" (the very not-rugged butter.

I tried hot water and then hotter water and then water that was no more than steam and would take the paint off of a tricycle, to no avail. I tried paper towels and then I tried my shirt and then I tried a dish towel, which I can only guess is made of material scientifically engineered to remove stuff from hands, all to no avail.

Finally, frustrated beyond words, I screamed, "What the fuck is with butter?! What in the Land of Lakes is going on? Why won't it come off my hands? What am I... toast?"

True story.

Even as the words left my mouth, I realized I'd blindly stumbled, in my unexpected outrage, on brilliance. If anyone else had been in the kitchen, their jaws would have dropped in appreciation of the moment, so I let mine drop three times further than usual. My mind felt like a freshly-blown nose. The steel had been poured, the only thing left to do was apply the hammer and tongs of editing (full disclosure: I originally typed thongs, which led to an image of an enormous, sweaty blacksmith standing at his anvil clad in nothing but leopard print. Given the sweltering heat of a furnace, I'm surprised more of them don't choose this option).

I knew I had to capture this profound thought (the quote, not the blacksmith in a thong) before it disappeared, but when I went to grab a pen, it flew out of my hands.

The butter.

The god-damned butter.

It got all over the paper I tried to write on. It got all over the keyboard of my computer when I tried to type. I wondered aloud why people say things are "butter" when they find them easy. I wondered aloud if next time I eat corn on the cob, I should forego the butter. I wondered aloud if "my mind felt like a freshly-blown nose" was a far better quote.

Still wish your mind worked like mine?

I thought not.

a grave situation

Finding the place proved to be just as tricky the second time. The small road leading to the old cemetery wasn't on the GPS and he only found it by making all the same mistakes he'd made the first time.

There was a chill in the air, over and above the typical chill that comes with being in a cemetery, a distinct difference from his first visit. November in Pennsylvania will do that.

He walked slowly to the headstone. When he got there, he bowed his head slightly and quietly said, "Hello again."

It had been spring two years ago when he'd last stood in front of the grave. He'd come there to ask the dead man permission to marry his daughter.

"Words mean something," he began. He'd rehearsed the speech over and over in his head on the three-hour drive to the cemetery but it still sounded weird to hear out loud. "They do. At least to me, sir."

There was a small town only a few miles away but he felt like he was standing a million miles away from civilization.

"I came here last time to tell you I loved your daughter. I did." A long sigh escaped from him. "I still do."

A large crow had taken an interest in the proceedings. To be fair, there wasn't much else going on, and it hopped closer and closer as the man spoke.

"I asked your permission to marry her. I thought it was important despite the fact that you're no longer with us… because you're still with her."

There was a rustling of leaves that hadn't been there in spring. It was like a sad soundtrack to the scene with the approaching bite of winter.

"I said something that day and I need you to remember it. I made you a promise and I need you to know I tried to keep it."

Monologues weren't his specialty. When you're emotional and alone and there's nobody there to listen but a crow and a corpse, it seems the very definition of a tough crowd.

"I said I'd take care of her as long as she'd let me." He'd added the last part without realizing it. Looking back, perhaps he'd known all along he wouldn't get the chance to keep his promise.

"She said no, sir."

The leaves stopped rustling and the crow stopped hopping. "I needed you to know I would have kept up my end of the deal."

He was holding a big yellow book. *Figuring* by Maria Popova.

"I'm sorry to say I don't even know if she's doing ok. I hope she is."

He opened the book to the page with the bent corner.

"Don't be mad at her sir. I was for a long time but it wasn't right to feel anger." He began to read, "Those accustomed to hard work and self-propulsion, who have risen to the zenith of accomplishment by force of will and magnitude of effort, are most susceptible to the supreme self-damnation of human life… the belief that love is something to be earned by striving rather than something that comes unbidden like a shepherd's song on a summer evening in the mountains of Bulgaria."

He was getting choked up until the word Bulgaria. He was thankful that Maria had included such a dumb-sounding location.

"So you see sir, it wasn't her fault. Everything I said about her last time is still true. You have an amazing daughter, sir."

There was so much more to say and yet nothing at all. He'd get no sympathy from a dead man. He shifted his weight from one foot to the other and closed the book.

"I guess I just wanted you to know. I'm sure she still thinks of you. I hope she still thinks of me."

Leaves blew across the grave but stubbornly refused to form a heart or smiley face. The crow had departed at the word Bulgaria.

"Take care, sir."

The man began the walk back to his car.

a showerly basis

Standing in the shower, all soaped up, I hear my cell phone ringing.

Do I answer it? Is it worth it?

Standing there thinking of all the wonderful news that could be waiting on the end of the other line.

Or the horrible news.

There would be hasty drying and inevitable dripping involved. Could I even reach it in time?

Maybe it's a wrong number… and what exactly do I mean by the word 'wrong?'

I met my first girlfriend because of a wrong number. She explained that she wasn't who I was looking for and I said "Not so fast…"

We talked and then we went to a movie and then she became the first girl who allowed me to experience "third base." I might be using quotation marks "wrong," especially right there where I actually meant wrong, but previously, and ironically, I was making a holistic point about the word "wrong."

I used a double quotation mark when talking about "third base" because I was young and inexperienced and it was a big deal at the time. If there was such a thing as a triple quotation mark, I would have certainly inserted it.

Is it a coincidence I used the word 'inserted'? If not, should it have been "inserted?"

I tend to use the word "holistic" whenever I can't actually make the point I'd set out to make so instead, I hope I made the point you needed me to make.

Standing in a shower is the perfect spot to wrestle with these important issues. All the while my phone sings its little song and what little shampoo is left in the bottle continues its tortuous climb down the side of the bottle. It was empty three showers ago, but I keep forgetting to buy more so I turn it upside down as soon as I enter the shower and only ten or fifteen minutes later, enough has succumbed to the forces of gravity to allow me to proceed with the head-washing festivities.

What would I consider good news? A call telling me that I've suddenly come into a large fortune.

And bad news? Perhaps a family member dying.

Or both. Is it 'wrong' to imagine that a long-lost relative on the other side of the world died peacefully in his or her sleep and left a massive estate to me?

With this newfound wealth, would I still have the shampoo problem I now face on a showerly basis? That question alone could keep me in the shower 'til my hands get all pruney.

What if it's the girl from the 'wrong' number all those years ago? Would I be flattered or nervous that she tracked me down after all this time? Could it be I'm better at "third base" than I am at fourth and fifth? With so much water under the bridge, I wonder if she could even pick me out of a lineup. I find myself hoping she could. It only seems fair that I know what it's like to get fingered.

What if, against all odds, she actually dialed me by mistake?

"Is Gary there?"

"No. This is Lance."

"Lance Manion?!"

"Yes. Why?"

"No way," followed by the unmistakable sound of a girl falling over, unconscious.

I finally have enough shampoo in my hand so I apply it and wonder to myself if there is, in fact, a sound that could not be mistaken for anything else but a girl passing out. Am I just lazy in my thoughts or does this sound exist? Would I make this very sound if I heard a long-lost relative on the other side of the world died peacefully in his or her sleep and left a massive estate to me?

Why do we shower? To get clean.

Why did I share all this nonsense? To come clean.

And, after all, I never invited you into my shower in the first place.

"Not so fast…" I hear you say. "Fifth base?"

take me back to the ballgame

I'm not a fan of baseball but I do admit that when I see the players wearing their "throwback" uniforms, it does fill me with a certain sense of nostalgia. A yearning for a simpler time when the "boys of summer" were the only game in town.

With this in mind, I think I'm going to approach Major League Baseball with the following idea: let's really embrace the spirit of the throwback game and broadcast it in black and white! Just imagine how cool that would look! It would be like stepping into a time machine.

And while we're at it, make the players use the same equipment they used back in the glory days.

As a compromise for having to use inferior bats and balls, players will be allowed to openly drink in the dugouts, including shots during the seventh-inning stretch.

Perhaps the marketing departments of each team can get their cities in the swing of things by enforcing a dress code for the game! Ties, jackets, and hats would be required to sit in the stands. Hopefully, the day will be a scorcher so the crowds can truly appreciate what their ancestors put up with when they made the decision to attend a game. While some might argue that heatstroke might detract from the overall enjoyment of the contest, on the plus side, each fan in attendance will either be given either a free carton of non-filtered cigarettes or a pouch of Red Man chew (14 years old and above only).

To give the day that added touch of authenticity, we could even give all of the black, Asian, and Hispanic players the day off! This should present no real problems… assuming all of the teams have a large number of minor league affiliates to draw upon to fill their rosters.

Before you jump to the conclusion that this is in any way racist, black, Asian, and Hispanics will obviously be allowed to attend the games! Of course, certain slight modifications to the stadium will be needed to ensure that the spirit of the day is not lost on the viewers (particularly drinking fountains and bathrooms).

The cherry on top of a magical day would be a quick shot of the player's wives hamming it up for the cameras.

Of course, some of the wives might not be exactly thrilled with the idea of having to dress up in the garb of the day but we will leave it up to the players to discuss it with them in the style of the day.

Did I forget to mention Cracker Jacks?!

Plenty of Cracker Jacks will be on hand.

Have I forgotten anything? I certainly hope not. I want to make sure my presentation to Major League Baseball is convincing. I sincerely believe that the "throwback" uniforms are just the tip of a very wistful iceberg.

Phil

Phil hates the left side of his car.

He demonstrates this by showing bias towards the right side. Every two years, he replaces two tires- the front right tire and the back right tire. Does he rotate the old ones to the left? No. Those are still the original tires. They are bald and you can see steel threads poking out.

He keeps the right side of his car immaculate. The left side? Not so much. When he gets the right side of his car washed, he carefully vacuums, creating a line of demarcation of sorts between the clean and the dirty.

Deep down, he believes the car is aware of his hatred of the left side. If he were to ever truly internalize the fact that his car was just made up of steel, aluminum, copper, rubber, and glass and held no opinion whatsoever on his feelings towards either side, being completely non-sentient, he would be bummed out.

He doesn't use the left side mirror and he taped over the left half of his rear-view mirror.

He has never replaced the left windshield wiper. When it rains, he's forced to lean over to look out of the right side. This makes braking difficult. At least the roads aren't slippery. Oh wait, they are.

He resents that he's forced to sit on the left side of his car to drive. He's envious of those countries where the steering wheel is on the right.

And the air vents on the left side of his car? Do I really have to tell you he keeps them closed? Are you even paying attention at this point? I'm guessing not.

Fucking oblivious.

You probably think this is come cleverly disguised commentary on political polarization. It's not. I'm trying to tell you about a crazy person named Phil.

He never signals when turning left.

But I do appreciate you trying to make this story into something a bit more interesting. It's not.

He disconnected the speakers on the left side of his car because AM radio is fine. He still gets to hear *"Brandy (You're a Fine Girl)"* now and then.

I realize my track record with metaphors and such but I swear, this is just a simple tale of someone who is slightly off.

He has gotten fourteen tickets over the years for having his front left headlight out.

I can almost see you, sitting there trying to figure out what else there is in a car I can possibly mention. Hoping to outwit me, getting a smug look on your face and saying to yourself "I saw that one coming."

The terrible truth is that his gas tank is on the left side of the car so he would slam the nozzle from the pump into the fueling receptacle quite roughly but eventually gave that up as it was becoming somewhat erotic in nature and so now he just slides it in gently. He's starting to struggle with that as well.

Didn't see that one coming did you?

Waiting for some "Phil her up" pun? Keep waiting.

He had half a sun roof installed. Guess which side?

Phil hates the left side of his car.

left and leaving

The two of them sat on the driveway, staring off into the distance. It looked exhausting.

"This driveway is attached to every road in the country. Like veins in a body. Cells and blood vessels. We could literally get in the car and go anywhere we wanted," said one of them.

"Which is?" said the other.

"Which is what?"

"What?"

I'm going to break in here before you lose interest and fast forward a bit. When you make dimwits the focus of a story, you run the risk of just this type of rocky start.

"If you could go anywhere, where would you go?" inquired the first.

"Who says I'd go anywhere?" answered the other. Proving staying put can be exhausting for everyone involved.

Trust me… I believe this story will go somewhere, so please hang in here. The interesting thing is how you picture these two. I didn't say their sex or race or where they are having this conversation. The two people pictured in your head are there with almost no prompting and I'll bet that if you would have started this story yesterday or even an hour in the future, these two would be significantly different. Changing faces that are always there.

"Within a few hours of driving, we could do something charitable or something terrible," said the first.

"Yeah. That's crazy," said the other, then continued. "This driveway leads to a road and that road leads to every other road out there. The possibilities. The endless possibilities. We could drive somewhere that leads to us getting rich or raped and murdered." They both took that thought in with equal parts awe and trepidation.

I insinuated they could drive, so I eliminated the fact that these two might be animals having a chat and I referred to them as "dimwits," so I bet that your own biases came rushing out to the forefront when picturing them. I'll let it go if you do. Wrestle with these prejudices on your own time.

"Makes you want to hop in the car and just head out, doesn't it?" said the one.

"Sometimes. Sometimes it makes me just want to sit here and picture all the possible outcomes of such a journey. Getting there might be half the fun but what's the other half? That's what I'd aim to find out."

The interesting thing remains how you picture these two. I didn't mention their sex or race or where they're having this conversation but there they sit in your head and by now, you've even filled in where they're sitting with quirky details that surprise you when you stop to take a longer look. Details that you might not have even meant to include but there they are nonetheless. Maybe that's why you enjoy reading. Maybe you're asking yourself a lot of the same questions they are and you resent me calling them dimwits.

"So what song would be on the radio as you headed out on your quest?" asked the one.

"I don't know. A good driving song, probably," answered the other.

I would suggest what the other would consider a good driving song but that could completely change them in your head and you could never get them back unscathed. Even inquiring what makes a good driving song could have people, both real and fictional, arguing for another thousand words. Throw in another five hundred debating how you can tell real from fictional and two hundred more asking if it makes a difference.

The other went on to ask, "Why? What song would be playing for you?"

"That's easy. I have a favorite driving song. It makes me drive faster and clutch the wheel and roll down the window and throw my head around like a moron."

Spoiler alert: I'm going to name the song and therefore probably change the scene you've created in your head because there *is* a song that makes *you* want to drive faster and clutch the wheel and roll down the window and throw your head around like a moron and this most likely isn't it but every story falls somewhere between getting rich or raped and murdered, so I suppose you have to take the crunchy with the smooth and endure the run-on sentences that transport you to every possible destination along the way.

"The song is 'Aside' by The Weakerthans," said the one. To show a requisite amount of enthusiasm, an imaginary wheel was grabbed, a head was thrown around and the following lyrics were belted out;

And I'm leaning on this broken fence

Between past and present tense

And I'm losing all those stupid games

That I swore I'd never play

But it almost feels okay

I must admit, I now regret calling them dimwits. A dumb premise suddenly becomes a bit poignant. Funny where some roads lead you.

Thanks for sitting shotgun awhile.

his name is Earl

Before there was Twitter and Snapchat, there was the CB (Citizen's Band) radio. Watch any movie made in the 70's and 80's that involved a trucker and I guarantee you that at some point, you'll hear his CB in the background spewing some colorful lingo. Lingo such as, "Bear In the Grass" (a police officer at a speed trap), "Bear In the Air" (a police officer in a helicopter or fixed-wing aircraft), or "Does a Bear Shit In the Woods?" (used when the answer to a question is obviously "yes").

That last definition was provided by Google. The same Google that defines "bear" as a term used by gay men to describe a large, husky man with a lot of body hair. So are they asking "Does a large, husky man with a lot of body hair shit in the woods?" That answer does not seem as obvious. If Google had been around in the 70's and 80's, I'm guessing a lot of movies would have been a lot more confusing.

All of which is my clumsy way of introducing you to Earl.

Earl is a long-haul trucker.

Honestly, thanks to Google, I've forgotten most of what I was going to say about Earl. I'll try my best to pick up my train (not truck?) of thought and press onward.

I don't have to describe him because once you read "long-haul trucker," you have already pictured him and nothing I can say will sway you from that image.

I can respect that and it makes my job much easier.

He has been married and divorced twice. Like many truckers, he has a mistress called the road.

A road that has led to Tonya (Memphis), Mona (Austin), and Carol (Portland) among many others. So really, the open road is his mistress… along with a lot of actual women.

He, as expected, buys all of his hats from convenience stores.

He firmly believes, not as expected, that Japanese babies cry in Japanese. He has spent many an hour debating the validity of this belief on his CB radio.

He stopped naming the dogs he travels with Lucky because they never end up that way due to the fact that truck stops include not only trucks that are stopped but trucks that are not as stopped and as soon as he christens a new dog Lucky, they quickly meet one of the not-as-stopped trucks, ending up not lucky at all. His latest dog, named Not Lucky, has been with him for a few years now and has avoided getting squished quite nicely.

He has a lot of time to think and he has used that time to write of some of the worst screenplays ever penned. And that's coming from me, someone who has written some of the worst books ever penned.

To give you an example, his movie treatment *Indian Summer Vacation* is about a bunch of geeky high schoolers on an Apache reservation who attend a summer camp and develop a rivalry with the camp of wealthy white kids across the lake.

There is plenty of romance, hijinks, and tomfoolery, some of the more awkward moments pulled directly from Earl's own experiences at summer camp as a teenager.

It ends with the white kids murdering all of the Indian kids and burning their camp to the ground.

Another screenplay begins with a close-up on a hard-boiled detective screaming at the top of his lungs... presumably because he's being immersed in boiling water.

Earl records all of his ideas for movies on a little recorder as he drives and then sifts through his various recordings at the end of every day, jotting down the good bits for later use. Not Lucky thinks he's talking to him so he wags his tail the whole time.

He remains persona non grata at the North Forty Truck Stop in Holladay, Tennessee for wiping off the last three letters on the restaurant whiteboard announcing "We Love Muffins."

A lot of men try trucking but leave the profession because it's a lonely lifestyle. That has never bothered Earl. He knows people in almost every town after all the years of driving and he always has his CB radio if he feels the need to talk to somebody. (Sort of makes you want to buy a CB radio doesn't it?)

People who use CB radios have "handles." Google defines a handle as a "nickname given or adopted by a CB radio user." Google the list of funny handles, it's definitely worth your time.

Earl's handle is Earl.

one terrible image for you

"Dad," began the boy. "You said I can ask you anything, right?"

"Of course," said the dad.

"Our dog is a girl dog, isn't it?"

"Yes, Lady is a girl," replied the dad, hoping that was the end of it.

It wasn't.

"Does she have a vagita?" the boy inquired with a serious look on his face.

"Yes son, she has a vagina."

"I rub her belly all the time and I've never seen it," the boy stated and gave his dad a look that seemed to indicate that further information would be required to wrap up the inquiry.

"Well, don't go looking for it," was all his dad could offer.

Unsatisfied with that answer, the boy continued. "Does it look like mommy's vagita?"

His dad laughed. "No. It does not look your mom's vagina. Can we stop saying vagina now?"

"No. You said I could ask you anything," his son said.

"Ok. What else do you want to know?"

The boy briefly stuck out his tongue and looked upwards in that adorable way children do when they are deep in thought. "Why doesn't it look like mommy's vagita?"

The dad gritted his teeth and grimaced in that adorable way men do before having an aneurysm. It took a few moments for him to collect himself. Finally, he said, "If dogs' vaginas looked like women's' vaginas, it would have definitely changed the course of human history. Especially important breakthroughs and discoveries."

The boy drew in a deep breath and waited.

"It would have gone," the dad raised one finger, "One: fire."

Obviously, he couldn't have verbalized a colon and, unlike quotation marks, you can't make "air colons" (although I think if you take the index fingers from both hands, stack them on top of each other and then make a poking movement forward that should make the point sufficiently) so just trust me when I say the colon was strongly implied.

He paused. "Then," holding up a second finger "Two: the wheel."

He took a moment to make sure he had the order right. "And then," holding up a third finger, "Three: pants for dogs."

Everything about the boy's expression said "And why would that be?"

The dad couldn't tell his son that if dog's vaginas looked like women's vaginas, men would probably end up fucking their dogs. He was too young for such information and would eventually grow up and learn this terrible truth anyway.

His son turned up the "Why is that?" volume on his facial expression to ten.

A single "Um" escaped the dad's lips before he continued. He was actually talking before he knew what words would be coming out.

"Well son, you see… if dogs wore pants… you know those women who carry around little dogs in their purses?"

His son nodded.

"If their little dogs wore little pants, then nobody would know if the carpet matched the corgi."

The dad seemed very pleased with this unexpected burst of wit. His face seemed to beam briefly before realizing that he was talking to a child and the reference would fly right over his little head.

The son looked more confused than ever.

"Pearls before swine," he grumbled.

"A swine is a pig," his son announced proudly. "Does a pig have a vagita too?"

"All girl animals have vaginas," the dad said, hoping to nip the line of questioning in the bud.

"Grasshoppers?"

"Probably."

"Is an elephant's vagita huge?" the boy asked.

"I would imagine it is."

Another long pause.

"Can we go try and find Lady's vagita?" the boy finally asked.

"Sure."

And that's how family pet boundaries get violated.

Love Street and Compromise Way

"So let me get this straight," the woman sitting with other grumpy-looking people behind a row of folding tables began, "You believe we shouldn't pave a road because it messes up a metaphor?"

"An analogy. Not a metaphor. But otherwise… yes," the man standing at the microphone replied.

"And you realize," she continued, "that will adversely affect hundreds of motorists on a daily basis?"

"Yes. That's sort of the point," said the man.

The woman leaned over and whispered something to the grumpy person on her right. People sitting in folding chairs behind the man began to quietly talk amongst themselves. It was chaos on a micro-level.

Sensing that the floor was now his, the man made his case. "Love is a bumpy road. It's rarely smooth and people shouldn't travel it unless they're ready to endure a few potholes."

"Yes, I understand, Mr. Johnson" (Mr. Johnson being the name of the man that until this moment has been referred to as "the man"), but this is a real road we're talking about."

"A real road called Love Street," he (Mr. Johnson) countered.

If you thought the first woman was grumpy-looking (let's call her Mrs. Fractural… an unfortunate choice I grant you but too late now), you should get a load of the man's puss (not Mr. Fractural, that would be pushing it. Their kid would be terminally grumpy. The doctor would take one look and say, "Congratulations Mrs. Fractural, you have a… holy cow! What a puss on this kid's face!" [an equally regrettable over-use of the word puss]) who spoke next.

"My colleague is being polite but we have a lot of topics to attend to this evening so, if you have nothing left to say…" he said in a manner as if to dare Mr. Johnson to not have nothing left to say.

He didn't. He didn't not have anything else to say.

Boy didn't he. He began by clearing his throat.

"Mrs. Fractural and other esteemed members of the Walcott Engineering and Economic Development department, I ask you to take the following under consideration." This would have been an excellent time for him to have mentioned something to consider but he was so relieved about remembering the name of their department that he lost his train of thought. The members of Walcott Engineering and Economic Development department all leaned forward as one, waiting for him to continue.

So he did.

"Our children will one day travel down this road, some idealized destination in mind, some circumstance urging them forward. Do we really want to miss this, and any other opportunity, to remind them that love is a bumpy road? Can it be impractical? Yes. Are there times it makes no sense? Sure. There are plenty of other ways to go that are easier, smoother. In fact, didn't you repave Compromise Way just last year?"

Most of the Walcott Engineering and Economic Development department members turned and looked at each other asking "Do we have a Compromise Way?" or "I don't remember funding a project of that name, do you?"

Not Mrs. Fractural. She was as sharp as a tack that had only been pushed into drywall a few times. She understood more than most where Compromise Way was located. Behind Mr. Johnson, other people began to sit up straighter and listen, their troubles with trash collection or the increased cost of cat licenses momentarily forgotten.

"Don't you see, members of Walcott Economical and Societal… I mean the Development of Economical Weights and Measures… Weights and Pulleys…" Mr. Johnson was fumbling and flailing now and Miss Rivers behind him had waited long enough to present her case about building a shed on her property to allow him to fumble out one more word.

"Mr. Johnson!" barked Miss Rivers, Mrs. Fractural, and the man seated next to Mrs. Fractural all at the same time.

"Why did I try to say their damn name again?" Mr. Johnson cursed himself under his breath. "It was going so well."

"Motion for grinding, repairing, and repaving Love Street, all in favor," announced Mrs. Fractural. Seven "ayes" were offered up and the motion passed unanimously.

Mr. Johnson walked out of the building smiling.

Why was he smiling?

Because Mr. Johnson and Mrs. Fractural had once been lovers.

She hadn't always been so grumpy.

the shower question

After overhearing someone complaining about how long someone else had been in the shower, punctuated with the observation "They're going to run out of water soon," it got me to thinking.

How large would the shower have to be to drain the Atlantic Ocean over the course of a typical ten-minute shower?

I would guess it would have to be miles high and definitely something you could see from outer space.

The question would be: could we build it? Do we have the technology and resources?

I know some of you would ask "Why would we want to?" but I would counter "Why not?" In a few billion years, the sun is going to absorb the Earth and extinguish all life as we know it, so what difference does it make how we spend the time?

Why not build an enormous shower that drains the Atlantic Ocean?

We would, of course, build it in the United States because this is just the type of "swing for the fences" project Americans love. It would put everyone to work. Just think of the plumbing needed. Miles and miles and miles of the stuff.

We'd start somewhere in the middle of the country, let's say Nebraska. We would need teams of engineers to figure out how to duplicate a shower that we all as Americans agree typifies the perfect shower, perhaps a poll could be taken in *Better Homes and Gardens*, and blow it up to the scale needed without losing any of its charm. I'm guessing that the footprint would take up most of Nebraska and might even bleed a little into Kansas. Once it got started and people saw the enormity of the task ahead of them, we'd need teams of politicians to remind them why it's so important that we build an enormous shower that drains the Atlantic Ocean. Would Mr. and Mrs. America buy in?

And then could we do it?

I mean physically do it.

Pump all of the water from the Atlantic, 82 billion billion gallons of water, into/through our shower. Think about it… a very daunting task. And then have the water drain into the Pacific.

If we could do it, I can almost hear the American President: "To the millions of men, women, and children in Asia that were swept away in what must have seen like an endless number of tidal waves and tsunamis, you have our sincere apologies. On the positive side of the ledger, however... we did it!"

A shower that can be seen from space and would eventually be stumbled upon by some alien race that would fly up to Earth just to take a closer look and wonder to themselves "What were they thinking? What needed washing that was so damned huge?"

Right there we would have accomplished something. Something *real* as a species. Meaningful.

An enormous shower that drains the Atlantic Ocean.

Sure, the sun is going to swallow it up eventually but until that time, it would be something we could be proud of.

An enormous shower that drains the Atlantic Ocean with nothing huge to wash.

I implore you to close your eyes and imagine it finished. Looking up at it. How it could possibly be built.

Just the scale of the undertaking makes my head spin. The pyramids? The Great Wall of China? The Chunnel? The Large Hadron

Collider? Child's play compared to the United States of an Enormous Shower That Drains the Atlantic Ocean.

Imagine the roar as 137 billion gallons of water fall from the sky every second when it's finally turned on. Niagara Falls? Please. That's only 75,000 gallons a second. This would be like 1.8 MILLION Niagara Falls.

If you've ever been to Niagara Falls, I think you're getting the picture. The enormity of it.

But could we do it? If every American puts all of their time and effort and money into it, make it a generational project, could we really build it?

I just don't know.

But we'll never know until we try and the first step to trying is giving it some serious thought. The more you truly think about it actually building such a thing the more you'll understand how I can't stop thinking about it.

It's overwhelming.

I'm overwhelmed.

Join me.

Nature 1, Lance 0

Don't get me wrong, I'm a big animal lover, but I've been having an issue with raccoons.

It started off as the usual tipped-over trash cans but has since escalated.

Twice a week, I put out my trash at the end of my driveway. I live in a pretty rural setting so it's not totally unexpected to have some woodland creature rummage through it from time to time. I consider it par for the course.

But these raccoons were different.

Starting a few months ago, these guys would make sure to tear up every single inch of garbage whether it contained food or not. So I upped the ante a little bit and bought new metal trash cans that had lids in hopes of dissuading them.

It did not.

In fact, it seemed to encourage them. I would get awakened in the depths of night by the sound of lids being banged together. It seemed to me they would wreak their havoc and then bang the lids together to celebrate. I would spring out of bed and charge down my driveway with murderous intent but the hairy villains would have already departed. Tucked safely away in the woods, I could still the see the gleam of their eyes watching me. Pinpricks of light that somehow felt ravenous, like stars sitting in the night sky. Twinkling but reminding me of the infinite darkness behind.

So I bought a 4-foot tall, 100-gallon locking heavy-duty stainless steel trash receptacle. It was magnificent as receptacles go. The first few nights I deposited the evenings refuse, I actually found myself sliding my hand up and down its sides affectionately.

"The CIA doesn't have trash cans like this puppy," I thought to myself proudly.

"Fuck those raccoons."

I remember staying up late, peering out the window, and watching them try to get at my garbage. Who could blame me if I purposely threw out a little extra food to sweeten the pot? Who could blame me if I Googled "raccoons favorite foods" and made sure that I packed 99.9 gallons of it into the 4-foot tall, 100-gallon locking heavy-duty stainless steel trash receptacle?

I'm just a man living in the middle of nowhere with a lot of time on my hands.

I should have figured it wouldn't end there.

I actually remember reading about the robbery at Home Depot but didn't think anything about it. I went about my day living in a fool's paradise. Me and my 4-foot tall, 100-gallon locking heavy-duty stainless steel trash receptacle.

That night, I heard a commotion and headed outside to gloat at the obviously frustrated efforts of my furry nemeses. And then what to my wondering eyes did appear? A raccoon sporting welding goggles sitting in front of my magnificent receptacle wielding the torch of a Tomahawk 1000, 60 Amp 230 Volt Plasma Cutter and his eight tiny companions.

Within seconds, and as I looked on dumbly, the side of my receptacle was compromised and out poured 99.9 gallons of fruit, poultry, nuts, vegetables, and eggs. I had even thrown in some uneaten lobster. They fell upon the contents of my violated receptacle like masked children on a ruptured piñata.

I could do nothing but stare, slack-jawed. I knew I had been beaten.

Any thoughts of acquiring firearms quickly dissipated as I thought about the careful planning that must have gone into the Home Depot heist. I knew in my gut they could easily pull off a similar stunt at a sporting goods store if weapons were needed. I saw no reason to escalate things any further.

I sat on my driveway and imagined little fingers pulling a little trigger and a little shiver ran down my spine.

It took three times of explaining to the garbage men that I wanted them to take away the 4-foot tall, 100-gallon locking heavy-duty stainless steel trash receptacle with the giant hole cut into the side of it - not just empty it. After they finally hauled it away, my original plastic trash can was back at its usual post.

But I'll tell you this much, those damn raccoons are never getting lobster again.

I have my dignity, after all.

seeds

"What's your name?" the comedian asked the nondescript man in the first row.

The comedian wasn't particularly famous or even well-known. It's not even certain that the nondescript man came to see this comedian or just was just there to see *a* comedian.

"Jerry."

Jerry sat back awaiting further questioning. Would it be about his job or where he was from or the woman who sat to his left?

The comedian smiled reassuringly. "Relax Jerry." The small audience laughed. They worried for Jerry. It was never good when a comedian picked you out of a crowd. The "Jerry" was always in for it.

"Do you remember what you were doing an hour ago, Jerry?"

Jerry looked at his date awkwardly and then stared off into the distance as if trying to remember. "We went to dinner," he finally answered.

"I was eating too, Jerry. Just down the road at IHOP. I like breakfast for dinner." The audience laughed again without knowing why.

"And what about this morning, Jerry? Where did you start your day?"

"At home. I live in New Brunswick. I like breakfast for breakfast."

The audience erupted in applause. Jerry was a hit.

The comedian laughed as well. "What about ten years ago?"

Still flush from his breakfast success, Jerry had to take a few breaths and try to remember where he'd lived ten years ago. Before he could answer, the comedian continued. "I was a salesperson in Wisconsin, Jerry. I hadn't yet gotten into comedy. I sold environmental cleanup services. And ten years before that, I was in junior high in Denver."

Nobody was laughing but the room was still friendly. Truth is, the comedian would have continued even if it wasn't.

"You see, Jerry, every decision I made, every friendship that began and ended, every job, every cookout, every birth, death, triumph, and tragedy was leading me right here, right now. Same with you, Jerry. Kind of makes it special, don't you think?"

Jerry nodded his agreement.

"Everything led to this moment between us, Jerry. Me talking to you." The comedian looked up and started to make eye contact with the other people in the room. "It's the same with everyone here. Every single one of you spent your lives getting here."

He let that sink in.

"Sort of makes me wish I was funnier."

Finally the audience had an excuse to laugh so they did. Relieved.

"I want you to imagine being thousands of feet above this club, looking down on it. Time lapse, an hour before the show. Watching everyone in the audience slowly making their way here. Being pulled from among everyone else. Walking in. Now rewind back ten years. You'll have to be miles above the club to stay with everyone. See us all distributed across the country, living our lives. Every interaction. Not knowing that eventually we'd all end up here. Being drawn inexorably to this single point in time and place. Everything having to be perfect to deliver us all but nobody having any other choice but to do the things necessary to be here right now. So many near-misses but we all got here. Intersecting lines."

The comedian could tell that some of the audience was wrestling with the idea of circumstance while others were debating the concept of fate. Others were bored and others were buzzed but they were all there.

"Now fast forward ten years until we're all in this club together… wishing I was funnier."

Laughter. A splattering of nervous clapping.

"Now get back above the club and fast forward ten minutes. We're all leaving. From above, it should look like blowing into a dandelion. The seeds floating and scattering." The comedian's attention returned to Jerry.

"What do you make of that imagery, Jerry?"

"So you're saying that we're the seeds and time is the wind…" Jerry offered up.

The comedian took his comment in and smiled. He seemed proud that Jerry had understood what he was saying." Exactly Jerry."

"I agree 100%…" continued Jerry, a small pause then, "Makes me wish you were funnier."

Zing! That Jerry.

the Zeitlin effect

In Eastern Pennsylvania, there are endless radio advertisements for a flooring company that features its owner as a trusted adviser on all things related to carpeting, hardwood, vinyl, and laminate. He's known as Norman the Floorman. He's a bit of a celebrity.

The name of the character in the following story is also called Norman. To complicate matters, he's also in the flooring industry. To be clear though, he is NOT Norman *the* Floorman. He is Norman *a* floorman.

To further elaborate, he is a foreman.

I will not drag this out any further by putting those two words together to elicit a cheap chuckle. Mostly because I'm pretty confident you'll do it anyway.

Norman looked up to see a very attractive woman about to sit down next to him. A welcome sight on any long flight. He could tell right away that she was not happy to be there. Her body language communicated that she was more than a bit apprehensive about flying.

Norman, a frequent flier, could not have been happier. Nothing endears a man to a woman more than offering comfort in times of distress. He saw this as his big chance.

As the plane taxied out to the runway, he glanced down to see her hand clutching the armrest in a white-knuckled fashion.

"Did you know that it is far safer to fly from Point A to Point B than to drive? It is by far the safest form of transportation," he began.

The ridiculously attractive woman looked up at him and smiled. "I'm a nervous flier. A touch of aviophobia, I'm afraid" was all she said.

"No worries at all. I'm here to talk you through it."

"Thank you," she relied appreciatively and gripped the armrest a little less intently. He offered her a piece of gum which she declined. "Helps your ears pop as you ascend."

Upon take-off, the plane rattled and shook a bit and Norman explained the physics behind what was going on, sprinkling in the word "lift" when needed. There's always a little comfort to be found in the notion of horsepower. This, despite the fact that horses don't fly.

The stewardess made the usual announcements but the fasten-seat-belt sign remained on despite Norman's prediction that it would be quickly doused.

The plane dropped sharply a few times and the woman next to him gasped and whimpered a little.

"Turbulence is no big deal. Think of it like a bumpy road. Like hitting a pothole. Nothing to be concerned about. Happens all the time," he said, trying to keep eye contact. His demeanor continued to be that of a man on a relaxing walk through the park. Casual.

The plane shook a few more times, each vibration more violent.

Then, about ten rows in front of Norman and the pretty woman, a large section of the roof ripped off.

"You'd be surprised how many times this stuff happens," Norman continued nonplussed.

In front of them, people were being sucked out of their seats and hurled into the yawning abyss. The noise of the wind and shearing metal grew deafening.

Norman began shouting, "The pilot will probably have to turn back around and land the plane now. Sucks."

That's when the plane began to spin wildly, their stomachs dropping and their brains trying to deal with the increased G forces. Debris swirled around the cabin. Screaming and calling out pleas to the gods for mercy seemed to be the most popular activities among the passengers.

Norman and the beautiful woman watched in horror as one of the wings snapped off and went in search of the folks who had departed earlier via the hole in the roof.

"It's hard… to… believe but… there have been…….. numerous people… survive falls… from much… greater…. heights than we…. no… doubt attained….. before………. this … slight…..hiccup…" Norman screamed into the attractive woman's ear.

During the shaking and rattling and whatnot, the button on the top of her shirt had popped open and Norman realized he had an unobstructed view of her upper boob.

The plane was tumbling towards the Earth in a complete free-fall at this point.

"I'm…. Norman …. I'm … a …………. floorman ……………. but …………………………………………………………………… not ………………………………………………………… Norman *the* ……………………………………………… floorman ………………………………………………………… just Norman …………………………………………… *a* floorman …………………………… did ………………… ………………………………………………………………… you ……………………………….want……………………… ………………………………………………………………… to ………………………………………………………… g e t coffee ………………………………………………………… ……………………………………………………… some ……………………………………………time?"

Before she could answer, they hit the ground.

how Miss Granch stole the 4th of July

Once upon a time, in a town very similar to the one you now live in, there was a middle-aged woman name Granch. Marcy Granch, to be more specific.

Marcy Granch was not a happy person. Because the author of this tale decided to make her a person instead of a made-up cartoon character, it is inappropriate these days to call her butt-ugly. If she was a Snorgel or a Drumpalump, then the author could tee off and say all sorts of horrible things about her appearance but, because she's human, let's just say she was manifestationally challenged.

She was as ugly as the word manifestationally.

On a side note, if any of you kids are looking for something wonderful to do when you grow up that would help society a very small amount but certain authors a great deal, think about creating a spell-check program for words that don't exist.

If you're saying to yourself "I don't ever remember reading a children's story that includes side notes," might the author suggest you stick your head in an oven?

One day, Miss Granch was watching videos on her computer. Outside, the winds were blowing and the rain was coming down in torrents but she sat all snuggled up with a cup of cocoa. After she finished a video about how to improve her self-esteem, she clicked on a video that was suggested to her by the site she was on.

If you're saying to yourself, "So you're telling me she's very open to suggestion," you have no idea how spot-on you are.

If you're now smugly saying to yourself "I'm pretty good at sniffing out plotlines," can we just make a deal that you stop saying things to yourself and just read the damn story?

The video she clicked on was of a hypnotist explaining how hypnotism works. "Fair enough," she said to herself.

Yes… *she* is allowed to say things to herself. She is in the story. You are not.

So eventually, the hypnotist asked her to stare at a spinning wheel on the screen and suggested that her eyelids would begin to get heavy.

"They are getting heavier and heavier. They are getting so heavy, you'll allow them to close," he said calmly.

Marcy Granch's eyelids, heavy as could be, closed.

"You are feeling very relaxed," the hypnotist continued. "Your eyes are closing tighter and tighter. You feel so relaxed that you feel your eyelids simply melt into your cheeks."

The howling winds outside, feeling a bit ignored, howled even louder but Marcy was far too relaxed to even notice.

The hypnotist snapped his fingers and Marcy felt a jolt run through her. "The more you try to open your eyes, the more they will stay shut. The harder you try, the more they will stay shut."

Marcy smiled to herself (and yes, you are allowed to smile to yourself… just keep quiet about it) as she realized it worked. She tried to open her eyes but couldn't.

And with one final heave, the wind and rain knocked over the necessary power lines and Miss Granch's house went dark. Except she didn't see it because her eyes were closed tight. All she knew was that the voice of the hypnotist was no longer with her and all she could hear was that sad little whimper a computer makes when it is shutting down.

Had she still been watching the video, she would have heard the hypnotist snap his fingers and tell her she could open her eyes. Instead, she sat there in the silent house unable to open them.

This story seemed to really impress a number of juries that heard it.

The jury who heard her legal case against the hypnotist.

The jury who heard her legal case against the website.

The jury who heard her case against the power company.

The jury who heard her case against the manufacturer of her computer.

You see, she was never able to open her eyes again! No amount of finger snapping seemed to be able to help. Doctors, therapists, and hypnotists all tried to work their magic to the best of their abilities and none of them could get Marcy to open her eyes.

The public was decidedly split on their opinions of Miss Granch as each new jury decision was announced. Each new decision making her wealthier and wealthier. Juries seemed to believe that each defendant was not only culpable in her sad state but that they had an unlimited amount of money to hand over to her.

If you're now thinking to yourself (scared to actually say it) "That's all well and good, but what does this have to do with the Fourth of July?"

First of all, thanks for just thinking it.

Second, remember the suggestion about your head and an oven?

Although Marcy Granch was now a wealthy woman, there was one thing she missed more than anything: fireworks. She loved fireworks. When she was a kid, she would lay awake on July 3rd with the same enthusiasm that most kids felt on the night before Christmas.

Now she could buy anything she wanted except the sight of fireworks going off in the night sky.

She opened and closed her hands repeatedly, each time bringing them into little fists. Her shoulders hunched slightly and a sneer crept across her lips.

Had anyone been there to witness it, they would have felt the little hairs on the back of their neck stand up on end.

She had an idea! An awful idea!

Miss Granch got a wonderful, awful idea!

"If I can't see them, nobody will," she hissed. For a moment, she fought the urge to throw her head back and let loose a loud maniacal laugh - she didn't want to frighten her cat.

With that, she began to contact every manufacturer of fireworks in the country to buy their inventory. She rented an enormous warehouse in Omaha, Nebraska and had everything shipped there.

All of the money she'd won was thrown into gobbling up every Peony and Blooming Flower. Every Roman Candle and Ariel Repeater. Every jingtinglern, floofloover, whohooper, and trumtooka. Every Girandola and Crossette.

And just as June was ending, she sent an army of workers across the country to wrestle away every last sparkler from super markets and convenience stores. Some of them physically taken from the hands of crying children.

And just as July was starting, newspaper headlines announced there were no fireworks to be had. Roadside stands sat empty. Firework displays were being cancelled left and right and television commentators collectively wrung their hands and blamed the current President and Global Warming.

Inside her hotel room in Omaha, Miss Granch danced around joyfully, fell over furniture and got up again, and hummed Granchily, "They're finding out now that no Fourth of July is coming!"

Oh, life is like that. Sometimes, at the height of our revelries, when our joy is at its zenith, when all is most right with the world, the most unthinkable disasters descend upon us. The phone in her hotel rang. It was her doctor telling her the results of her recent medical exam were back: they indicated she was suffering from dilated cardiomyopathy and was at a high risk for congestive heart failure.

"Dilated cardiomyopathy is an enlarged heart!" you are no doubt saying to yourself, so proud that you caught the "heart grew three sizes that day/Grinch" inference, then wondering to yourself "was the full *Christmas Story* quote really necessary?"

Either way, the news of her mortality really opened Marcy Granch's eyes. Literally and figuratively. She could see and for the first time in years, she could *see*!

"I must get these fireworks back into the stores," she announced to nobody and asked her chauffeur to pull up the car. She pushed him out of the driver's seat and roared off to the warehouse. She would make things right if she had to drive every whistlin' bunghole, spleen splitter, cherry bomb, or slooslunka to an open field and set it off herself.

Unfortunately, it had been years since she'd been behind the wheel and her depth perception was still a little shaky so just as she was going through the front gate of the warehouse, she lost control of her vehicle and sent it crashing into a crate of blumbloopas.

The resulting explosion was seen from the International Space Station and most of Omaha was left a smoldering ruin.

I said I'd never miss you, but I guess you'll never know
Where the bridges I have burned never really led home
On the fourth of July
-Fall Out Boy

his road to ruin

It started when he was young. The first time was at a steakhouse. It was crowded. It must have been some minor holiday or other as it was packed and noisy and as he was sitting in the booth with his family, he closed his eyes. When he opened them, he was alone. The restaurant was dark and completely empty.

As if he was sitting in the same place just later that night, long after it had closed. Something hung in the air but he was too young to understand what. He could feel his heartbeat in his ears.

He looked around and noticed details. Torn fabric on the chairs and the same bad pictures hanging on the walls. Lights from a passing car quickly moved across the tables, making the napkin holders twinkle for a second or two, and then disappear again. It was completely quiet.

Until it wasn't… and the soundtrack to his meal came flooding back along with everything else. He was back in front of his sirloin.

A few years later, it happened again. At the county fair. He was standing in line for the tilt-a-whirl with his friends and then he wasn't. He was standing on an empty fairground. The rides and the people and the dizzying lights and obnoxious music were all gone.

There was a light breeze and he saw the grass gently swaying. There were birds in the background and he knew he was in the same spot just at a different time. It wasn't just a black-and-white picture, although he'd later remember the colors as seeming a bit subdued; he was there. It seemed real. He just felt like it was a few weeks after the carnival had left town.

He took a step forward -in the restaurant, he'd sat frozen in his seat- and felt the ground under his feet.

He walked to the empty parking lot and then retraced his steps, scared he'd get lost.

"Where did you go yesterday?" his friends would ask him later.

"I got separated," was his reply. He did not elaborate.

On his twenty-first birthday, he found himself standing outside his own front door, knowing that everyone he knew was on the other side waiting to yell "Surprise!" and he briefly fantasized about walking in to find it empty. Imagining everyone's surprise when the door swung open and there was nobody behind it.

He squeezed his eyes closed, opened the door and everyone yelled "Surprise!" and he acted surprised.

The incidents ended when he was in his mid-thirties. He worked in the city, in a big high rise. Just as before, there were no warning signs. He was walking down the hall and then the hall looked different. Everything looked different. Smelled different. Of decay.

It wasn't just a few weeks later, it felt like much longer.

Much longer.

The building was dilapidated. Crumbling. There were gaping holes in the walls and mildew covered everything. Water dripped from X to Y with no concern for Z.

His forward momentum carried him further down the hallway until he came to the stairs. The same stairs he'd taken a hundred times before, but never with the fear that they would collapse under his weight. He noticed the hairs on the back of his neck weren't standing up as they'd been during the earlier episodes (including the surprise party).

When he was on the street, he looked around and saw a ruined city. Completely deserted.

Not as if it were *the* future but as if it was *a* future.

He bent down and ran his hand along some of the grass poking up through what was left of the sidewalk. It felt nice on his palm. That was the only thought in his head.

He walked on, no longer sacred of getting lost.

Back at the office, they wondered where he was.

"I think he was headed towards the copy room," someone offered.

A few weeks later, everyone wondered where he was.

13C

It started with a rattle that grew into a violent shuddering, followed quickly by screaming and tumbling and smoke and fire and then, absolutely nothing. Sort of like how I imagine it when a wave crashes over a surfer... except with more smoke and fire. And, of course, the screaming.

I don't want to understate the role of the screaming that went on.

I've never surfed- too late for the bucket list now- but I picture a few seconds of complete silence before things start to rush back to you.

Silence and blackness and then, I was back in my seat. 13C. An aisle seat.

"Ladies and gentlemen, this is your Captain," came a voice over the speakers - a pretty damn impressive Captain voice. There weren't horns blasting in the background when he made his announcement, but I felt them anyway.

The impressive Captain voice continued. "I regret to inform you, there has been a terrible accident and you're all deceased."

This came as a bit of a blow to many of the passengers on the Boeing 757-2Q8. As if on cue, there was a ping and the little overhead sign saying that we needed to keep our seatbelts on turned off.

Were we free to move about the cabin? Nobody did.

(I feel it's important to point out that while I'm writing this, I am listening to the *Explosions In the Sky* album *All Of A Sudden I Miss Everyone*. Why is this important? I'm not sure... it just is. Is it important you listen to it as you read this? Only you can answer that.)

I realized I was still gripping the armrest like my life depended on it. When I realized that it didn't, I let go and flexed my fingers a bit.

"If you'll be patient, we will have you on your way to your final destination shortly."

This news was not well-received.

Final destination?!

We all started to look at each other nervously. Was this some sort of shared hallucination?

"Please tell me this is a bad dream," someone said a few rows behind me. Behind her, someone began to weep softly. I realized that I still had an unopened bag of almonds that the flight attendant had given me mid-flight. With all that was going on, I thought it odd that I was thinking about nuts, but there you have it.

I watched the man sitting next to the window stare out and say "We really are dead." I wondered what he was seeing and wished for a second he'd move his big, dumb head. Then all of a sudden, I wished I hadn't had a mean thought.

The timing seemed particularly bad.

The door to the cockpit opened and a man walked out. He looked like every pilot that has ever appeared in an American Airlines commercial. Steely, blue eyes (that I could somehow see clearly from 13C), a square jaw, and surrounded by a warm light. He smiled and I was filled with a strange calm.

"I'm sorry for the inconvenience. I'm sure you all had important places to be, but unfortunately, Eric Lloyd Cleese in seat 27B didn't put his tray table up as instructed." He then mouthed the word "Boom" and opened both of his hands to mimic an explosion.

Before our most charismatic Captain could continue, Jeffery Allen Holmes in 28A burst out, "You filthy cocksucker!" and attempted to lean over and rain blows down on Eric Lloyd Cleese. Sally Louise Jefferson in 28C tried to stop Jeffery Allen Holmes from raining blows down on Eric Lloyd Cleese as Mark Joseph Masterson in 28B put his head in his hands.

I finally got a look out the window and saw grainy black and white footage of my life rolling by.

"Please check around your seat for any personal belongings you may have brought on board with you and please use caution when opening the overhead bins, as heavy articles may have shifted around during the flight," our Captain said.

The people up front began to stand and file out.

"A gate agent will meet you as you depart to direct you to your final destination. Please be aware that some of you might have an unscheduled layover between a few days up to fifty-thousand years. On behalf of whatever airline this was and the entire crew, I'd like to thank you for joining us on this trip. Have a nice afterlife."

I smiled to myself as I watched some people grab their carry-on (with a "better safe than sorry" air) and some people leave them behind (was that a devil-may-care attitude I detected?). Behind me, Jeffery Allen Holmes must have realized that striking Eric Lloyd Cleese was going to have him sitting in one hell of a layover, so he was making the most of every punch.

"How does a tray table being down cause a plane crash?" wondered Eric Lloyd Cleese to himself between blows.

I stood up. Those in front of me were moving forward with varying degrees of composure. I reached down and grabbed my nuts. Ahead, I could see the exit.

The Captain was nodding to everyone as they passed. When I was standing in front of him, I leaned in and said "That was a really shitty landing," and laughed. He put his arm around my shoulder and replied "Why do people who refer to death as passing to the other side always assume that there's only one other side?"

"Will I be needing these?" I asked, holding up my nuts.

"You might at that."

systemic stupidity

Systemic is a word you hear a lot these days. Mostly because it's an impressive word. It makes the people saying it feel like they're smarter than they are.

Systemic: something that is spread throughout, affecting a group or system, such as a body, economy, market, or society as a whole.

Feel free to stop and use it in a sentence if you need a quick boost of self-esteem.

The word following it in most cases is "racism."

Systemic Racism –something that is blamed when a bunch of dipshits decide to start looting and burning stuff down.

There's no such thing. It's a myth. In the case of people burning stuff down, they are just society's losers. The angry and unhappy. To try and blame it on skin color or sexual orientation or any of the other almost-infinite things that make us different is just dipshittedness.

Do you have any idea how many things can be blamed for an individual's lack of success?

Do you have idea how hard it is for blind people in this society? Anyone can see, that *can* see anyway, that everything is built for people who can see! And you don't see blind people rioting, do you?

And if you did, they certainly couldn't.

And height. There has been study after study showing that the taller you are, the greater advantages you enjoy in our society. And you don't see midgets rioting, do you?

Although, you have to admit… it would be hysterical.

"Sergeant. The midgets have looted the Piggly Wiggly!"

"How do you know it was them?"

"Everything on the top two shelves is untouched."

"Yep… that's midgets alright."

Ugly people have always had it rough. Maybe the roughest. Ugly people, whatever color they are or however they identify, are at the bottom of the food chain in our society and yet nobody says a word about it. I know a lot more white women with black friends than I do attractive women with ugly friends.

If they rioted, you know the newscasters couldn't wait to say, "It's really getting ugly out there."

Fat people! You can't throw a rock without hitting a fat person these days. Like the ugly, they are wildly under-represented in TV shows, movies, pop music, fashion shows, and Fortune 500 boardrooms, but nobody says a word. Nobody cares or fights for their "rights."

And believe me, if you want to see a Piggly Wiggly looted properly… send in the fat people.

It's just black skin that we need to worry about, right? Despite the fact that blacks in the US have never been more prosperous or enjoyed more advantages than they do today.

I can hear you saying to yourself, "But wait, Manion! Some people don't like them because of the color of their skin. They don't give them the same opportunities."

No shit.

But when was the last time you saw a college give preferential admission treatment to an ugly person or a fat person or a midget? Add skin color to the laundry list of reasons why some people don't like other people. The witty vs. the dull. The people with a full head of hair vs. the bald. Good singers vs. people who can't carry a tune. Healthy vs. handicapped. Type A people vs. the lazy.

Don't get me started on ageism in this country. Do you really want to see a riot made up of people over the age of 80? Do you know how many hips would get broken?

"Sergeant. It's the Piggly Wiggly again! The old folks have looted it!"

"How do you know it was them?"

"The only things taken were Metamucil and hard candies."

At the end of the day, you shouldn't ask yourself why people loot stores. You should wonder why everyone doesn't always do it. Obviously, there will never be enough police to control crowds if everyone decided to just go to the mall and take stuff.

So, why don't we? Why do we pay for things in the first place?

Because it works best for everyone. It's what separates us, black & white & tall & short & ugly & handsome & fat & skinny, from Third World countries. The key word being US. What we've all agreed upon, our culture, has created more prosperity and happiness than any other civilization in the history of the world. It works.

You get educated. You contribute. You roll the dice and hope for the best. You pay for things and hope that the losers that make up Antifa get run over by cars driven by fat, ugly midgets.

I mean, they can barely see over the dashboard.

(If you don't take a moment to visualize each of the various groups mentioned rioting and looting, then you're really missing out. A handicap riot? Are you kidding me? I could picture that all day. The parking would be a nightmare.)

simple

Everything is a story. Everything is a song. So simple. Beautiful.

Except this.

She was willing to give me what I wanted, a proper goodbye. A romantic send-off. One last time to say all the things we wanted to say. To touch. One final time to make love. Connect.

This is what I asked for and this is what she agreed to and this is what I wanted and longed for and this was the reason I was at her door.

And couldn't knock. My hand felt like it was made of lead. I couldn't lift it.

I realized I'd rather leave things with the possibility of being rekindled, however slim those odds might be, than end them perfectly.

Until that moment, I didn't think anything could be as hard as not knowing. Spending days and weeks and months apart. Were we or weren't we? Knowing I was… was she?

I thought if we could end it like a movie, I'd somehow be able to live with it. One transcendent memory.

What a load of shit. When it ended, it would be over. Truly over after so many close calls. I'd have to walk out the door and never return. I would trade a dozen romantic endings for one real shot to be with her forever.

So I turned around and got back in my car and drove away.

From her. From the perfect ending.

So that I could spend that night alone, waiting for the call or text that I knew wouldn't come.

And the next night, staring up at the stars.

And the next, tossing and turning.

And the next.

And the next.

Maybe that's how you know.

I wouldn't trade her for anything… not even her.

So simple.

Maybe everything is a story after all.

Detective Ferguson needs a hand

"When you have eliminated all which is impossible, then whatever remains, however improbable, must be the truth."
—Sherlock Holmes

Detective Ferguson had a problem that made him want to throw his hands up in the air. All nine. His two and the seven other ones that sat on his desk.

Seven severed hands, the result of a serial killer that had been on the loose in his city for three months. He had no leads. He had no clues. His contacts at ViCAP (Violent Criminal Apprehension Program) had nothing for him. He'd watched *Silence of the Lambs* twice but he couldn't find anyone currently incarcerated that had dabbled in severed hands.

He would have settled for any severed limbs really; he was just out of luck in that department.

I'll skip ahead to the part where he gets so desperate that he considers an even more extreme measure. Just know he was not happy about it and didn't share what he was about to do with anyone else at the station.

After the last officer had left the building for the night, he loaded the seven hands into an Igloo cooler and left clandestinely out a back door where he knew there was no video surveillance.

Incidentally, the cooler was his "lucky" cooler. Since his divorce four years ago, his dating life was hit or miss, but whenever he suspected a "hit" was on the horizon, he would invite a girl on a picnic. That was where he did his best work. Put him on a blanket in the woods and he was going to close the deal. Wine, cheese, grapes, all carried inside the same container that now held seven severed hands.

He put the address into his GPS and headed out to meet the palm reader he'd found online. He arrived five minutes early for his appointment and sat in his car trying to figure out how he was going to approach the next few minutes. It was a wasted five minutes. The purple glow of neon coming from the Palm Readings sign in the window didn't help.

"What the fuck am I doing here?" he asked himself as he got out of the car and headed for the door.

Moments later, a woman opened the door. He was not disappointed by her appearance. It was right out of central casting. The flowing dress, the gypsy headdress. The whole shebang.

Madam Lauren led him inside to a small table. All around him hung beads, crystals, and posters illustrating the human hand in all its glory. Incense hung in the air.

He put the cooler on the table with a thud.

"I need you to take a look at some hands," he began.

She smiled and said "That's my job."

"I don't think you understand…" and with that, he opened the cooler.

She peeked inside then took a step back, the color draining from her face. Before she started screaming and fleeing into the night, he thought he'd better explain.

"I'm Detective Ferguson. These are the hands of the victims of a serial killer we're trying to catch. We're at a dead end and I need your help." He gave her his most sincere look. An awkward silence fell over the room. Fearing he was losing her, the detective continued.

"I can't say I believe in all this stuff," he gave a quick wave around the room, "but as I said… we're stumped."

Madam Lauren took her first breath since seeing the contents of the cooler. "I'll have to charge you per hand, you realize."

"I thought this was more of an hourly rate thing," Detective Ferguson started but quickly realized he did not have the upper hand in this negotiation. Haggling would not be appropriate. He smiled an uncomfortable smile and took out the first hand. "And don't tell me that this man met a violent end. I got that much."

"I'd like to start with yours, if you don't mind," she said.

"Listen, I didn't do it, so I don't see the point…" he began, but she cut him off. "If you want my help, then you'll do as I ask."

The detective put the hand back in the cooler. "I think this was a mistake," he said and put the lid back on a little too forcefully.

"It's your call, detective, but if you want to solve this case, it's not going to be a picnic." She put a particular emphasis on the last word.

He sat down and extended his hand.

blood

It started with a small cut on his arm.

He'd been in the yard, cutting back some of the vines and shrubs in his garden and a thorn had, unbeknownst to him at the time, lodged in his arm. It wasn't until his wife saw the little bloodstain that he was even aware of it.

She made it seem like he'd been wounded in hand-to-hand combat. She washed it, applied some antibacterial and a Band-Aid. He had to admit he enjoyed the attention.

The next time he was gardening, he didn't purposely injure himself, but let's just say that he wasn't as careful when he went by the rose bushes as he usually was. When he was done with his little journey through the Celine Forrestiers, Harison's Yellows, and Fakir's Delights (roses by any other names), he sported two scratches that put his previous wound to shame. Blood trickled from each.

He couldn't wait for his wife to see them.

It took a couple of nonchalant walks past her before she eyed them, but once she did, she once again leapt into action with a gusto that would have left Florence Nightingale impressed. While the antiseptic stung a little, he basked in the concern his wife displayed.

This little scene began to play out on a regular basis until his wife started to suspect something was amiss. Nobody could get scraped or punctured every time they stepped outdoors. It dawned her one day after she tripped and sprained her ankle. As her husband jumped up to help her to a chair, she suddenly understood and smiled to herself.

It *was* nice.

Realizing he might have overplayed his hand a bit, he took a few weeks off from his injurypalooza. But he was not done.

Far from it.

It was a quiet Saturday morning and attempts to run over his foot with the mower ended poorly. Only the tops of his sneakers were affected. Scratch one pair of ASICS Gel-Venture 7 shoes.

Not one to give up easily, he turned the mower on its side and removed what was left of his right sneaker. He lifted up his foot and placed it in the still-running mower.

He let out a scream. Inside the house, at precisely the same time, his wife let loose a terrible shriek and his dog unleashed an anguished howl and his parrot an unholy squawk. If his hearing had been good enough, he might have also picked up on a ruckus in the vicinity of the fish tank.

With blood fountaining out of what remained of his right foot, he began to hop and hobble towards his front door. The driveway and front steps were bright red and getting redder. As he opened the door, his wife met him, tears streaming down her face. Through the center of her left hand, which she held up for inspection, was a long knitting needle. Blood poured out of both sides of her hand.

Behind her, the family dog had somehow gotten his food bowl wedged in his own ass and behind the dog was the parrot, completely impaled on his metal swing.

Feathers floated down peacefully underneath the cage.

Even though the man considered himself a good pet owner, he didn't have the heart to look in the fish tank.

The edges of his vision began to get black. He was losing a lot of blood and on the verge of passing out. His wife looked a bit pale herself and lost her footing on the slippery entryway. The ankle returning to a state of sprainedness as a result.

His dog was walking around like a cowboy.

The parrot twitched on the newspaper, uneaten seeds adding a tiny rustling accompaniment.

A good foot away from the tank, the fish flopped around on the carpeting, unnoticed.

I guess deep down, I'm hoping that amongst my readers is one that recognizes and appreciates that Celine Forrestiers, Harison's Yellows, and Fakir's Delights are roses known to have particularly nasty thorns.

Trevor sees a sunrise

There was no one event in particular that made Trevor realize he'd never truly witnessed a sunrise. Obviously, he'd been up when the sun was rising hundreds of times over the course of his life, but he'd never anticipated it and given it his complete focus. Once this realization was made, he knew this oversight must be corrected in all haste.

So the next day, he slept in late and ate a healthy dinner and when the sun was ready to set, he braced himself for what was sure to be a long night. A long night that would end with a sunrise.

He couldn't have picked a better night. It was early summer and the temperature was nice enough that he wouldn't even need a jacket. He could stroll leisurely into a nearby nature preserve and spend the night hiking up the side of a small mountain so that at the appropriate time, he'd have a front row seat for the big reveal.

About an hour after the sun had disappeared below the horizon, he craned his neck up and really looked at the clouds. He drank them in. Up until that moment, he'd never drunk in a sky. The clouds looked like a cross between a quilt and the skin of an old giraffe he'd seen at the zoo. If that giraffe had sported a fluffier pelt. The longer he looked up, the bigger the sky got until it was enormous and he felt a bit dizzy. He'd drunk in too much sky.

The giraffe skin made him remember a trip to the zoo he'd taken with an old best friend. They had seen a camel whose beleaguered hump had fallen and was just laying on its back and he told his friend that it was because the camel was unhappy. His friend corrected him and said that he was thinking of killer whales.

"Oh, you're right," Trevor had replied. "They hate captivity."

"We're all captives to some extent," said his ex-best friend whose name would eventually come to him. He'd said it very casually and with no drama and they moved on to the pandas.

Surrounded by trees, there's always a small rustling noise going on somewhere. Be it the breeze or an unseen animal, there's always something to listen to.

At about ten o'clock, he remembered that when he was a kid, he'd been so impressed with a classmate's drawing of a dragon, he'd bought it from him and then told his mother that he'd drawn it. She didn't believe him for a second and it infuriated him.

"Why couldn't I have drawn this?" he asked her.

"That's not how you draw," she said tactfully.

"Well, you're wrong. I drew this," he replied defiantly.

His mother got up from the table and returned with a piece of paper and pencil. "OK then. Draw me a dragon."

Almost immediately, he'd regretted trying. His dragon was awful. He was an awful artist and this dragon was starting off particularly awfully. About a third of the way through its dopey-looking face, he abandoned the effort and stormed off.

Trevor took a deep breath and realized how much he missed his mother. To have someone who cared enough about you to know how your terrible dragon would look before you even drew it was something that doesn't come along a lot in life.

Somewhere in the distance, an owl hooted.

The clouds that looked like fluffy giraffe skin had moved on and now the sky was clear. Really clear. Crazy clear. He felt like he was standing on a rock floating in the middle of a black abyss. Everything dropped away except the little points of light that he knew were in fact giant balls of burning gas billions of light years away. He suddenly missed his giant ball of burning gas.

At about one o'clock, he realized his ball of gas was still burning away and if he were only on the other side of 7,917 miles of rock, he could feel its warmth on his face. Instead, he was facing the wrong way and a small chill ran through his spine. The dark has its charms, but he missed the light.

At two o'clock, he remembered a time when he dropped his pen while working. He looked down but couldn't find it. Instead of just getting a new black pen, he scoured the cream-colored carpet under his feet. He scooted around in his chair, looking. It had to be there somewhere. It wasn't. He began to move furniture, intent on finding it. Had he imagined dropping it? Had he imagined he'd been working? Eventually, he found the pen behind his desk. It was impossible though. There was no way it could have bounced or rolled there. No way at all. He never figured it out and now he wondered if he'd just imagined the whole thing.

At about three o'clock, he remembered an old girlfriend who would talk in her sleep but only moments before waking up, so most mornings started off confusing; he was forced to admit to himself that he didn't know if he wished her well or not. He liked her and they parted ways mostly (about 83%) friendly, but when he thought about her being happy without him, it hurt a bit. When he thought about the possibility that she was unhappy, it also hurt. No wonder he buried his emotions whenever he had the chance.

"You don't see rock or balls of gas getting so conflicted," he said to himself.

He arrived at the top of the mountain, which anyone who was familiar with real mountains would definitely think of as a hill, in plenty of time. Crickets provided the soundtrack. He'd spent the night wandering through a forest, which anyone who was familiar with real forests would definitely think of as the suburbs, alone with his thoughts and he was ready to wrap things up.

He sat down, cross-legged and waited. Excited.

Finally, it started.

A purple glow that slowly turned red. Orange made an appearance and suddenly, the entire horizon was on fire.

And slowly, his eyes adjusted and he saw it.

A single shaft of light.

His long night was almost over.

The sun.

His world was turning (at a thousand miles an hour).

He realized he was crying.

in yodeling and in health

A little background will help. If you don't see the whole picture, you might feel I'm not being reasonable. Once you see the whole picture, there's still a chance you'll feel I'm not being reasonable.

Reason, like so many things, is overrated.

Every Saturday morning, I make myself French toast and a cup of English Breakfast tea. It's the highlight of the weekend. Before I start this weekly breakfast ritual, I perform another one. A daily ritual. I go downstairs and give my dog a treat. Day in and day out. Even if I'm in a bad mood and even on mornings following some doggy transgression the previous evening.

Every. Morning. Like clockwork.

So on Saturday mornings, it's a treat for the dog and then the breakfast ritual.

The cornerstone of the breakfast ritual being the four songs I listen to. They are every bit as important as the eggs and bread. Four John Denver songs: *"Calypso," "Rocky Mountain High," "Take Me Home Country Roads"* and *"Thank God I'm a Country Boy."*

I have the actual preparation of the French toast and cup of tea down to a science. Swiss watchmakers would look on in envy as I load the last piece of French toast onto the plate as the final chorus of *"Thank God I'm a Country Boy"* winds down. I imagine watching me beat eggs and add sugar to my tea would be akin to watching Olga Smirnova dance a ballet around her kitchen. Grace in motion.

Ok. I think the background has been established. I can now move on to the point of this.

I had sort of noticed this a few times in the past, but I was happy to write it off as a coincidence. You know what I mean; facing a hard truth is sometimes difficult, so people tend not to see what they don't want to see.

But this morning, I paid attention, and I saw.

And my heart broke.

Early in the French toast-making process, as *"Calypso"* started getting down to brass tacks, I looked over at my dog. Then came the chorus. A chorus that involves a little yodeling.

So I began, as I'd done countless times before, a full-throated yodel.

My dog left the kitchen.

Let me repeat that. The dog, who I have spent countless hours walking and cleaning up after and giving treats to, turned and walked away from me.

Over a little yodeling.

Man's best friend, my ass!

She'd been doing it every damn week. Abandoning me when things got tough. I suddenly had flashbacks, like they do in all those murder-mystery movies, of seeing her stand up and walk out every time I started yodel-oh-ee-deeing.

Et tu, Daisy?

I don't know what the Saturday breakfast/dog landscape is going to look like next week. Would I want my post delivered by a mailman who lived by the credo "Neither snow nor rain nor heat nor gloom of night stays these couriers from the swift completion of their appointed rounds. Just yodeling. Yodeling stays them"?

I do know that if that mailman is expecting belly rubs the next time I see him, he's in for a rude awaking.

Do I sometimes slap my knee and pretend I'm wearing an invisible cowboy hat when I sing along to *"Thank God I'm a Country Boy?"* Yes. Yes, I do. I'm an imperfect creature.

But you know who has never seen that show?

My own dog! My pal. My best friend.

She bails at the first yodel-oh-ee-dee.

I realize I promised a point to all this so here it is: I look adorable when I'm slapping my knee and pretending to wear an invisible cowboy hat.

Your loss, dog.

that's when it hit me

It was a great slap. Anger transformed into a long graceful arc of her arm. Her palm catching me flush in the face. Textbook form. Despite my need to remain composed, a single tear escaped my right eye and made its way down my burning cheek.

I had made a comment I shouldn't have, but it was out before I could corral it.

She'd had a relative pass away. A relative that was "intellectually disabled." I wanted to offer words of solace, but the first thing that popped in my head was how relieved I was that, because of the self-quarantining going on, we wouldn't have to go to the funeral. She was unamused.

Then she became really unamused when I added, "What would anyone even say at the eulogy? Bring up moments when she was particularly retarded?"

Slap.

I don't know why I said it out aloud. I'm a horrible person, but usually I can keep it under wraps.

Later, trying to make lemonade from lemons, I told her how impressed I was with her slap. She was a natural slapper. With some training, I said I thought she could be a champ.

Later that same day, almost on cue, I ended up reading about slap-boxing, a sport where open handed slaps are used instead of fists. The article mentioned that the Russian champ Vasily Kamotskiy would be headlining an upcoming tournament only a few towns over.

Amateurs were welcome to enter and compete.

That got me to thinking…

Soon, I was helping my girlfriend train. Morning, noon, and night. It was right out of a *Rocky* movie. Raw eggs and everything. I explained that it wasn't the size of the person slapping, it was all in the form. She is a total "women's empowerment" fan, so I got her believing that she could out out-slap anyone, male or female. In fact, being a girl, they would probably go easier on her and she could make them pay for such condescension.

It was all very exciting. I had made her a believer.

The day of the tournament, we got up early and watched *Karate Kid IV* to get her in the mood. Girl power! After a healthy breakfast loaded with carbs, we jumped in the car and headed over to the rec center that was holding the contest.

The parking lot was packed. I guess this Vasily Kamotskiy was a bit of a celebrity even here in the US.

What's great about slap boxing is you don't have to buy gear or wear anything special. Just show up and start slapping.

My girlfriend's first match was with a mountain of a man. Easily 300 lbs., arms ripped from the pages of *Excessively Muscular Magazine* and sporting a lumberjack beard that made him look like he had some grizzly bear DNA in him somewhere. I certainly wouldn't have wanted to be standing in my girlfriend's shoes.

Unfortunately, the massive gentleman won the toss and would be slapping first. He reared back and let loose with a viscous blow that took my girlfriend's head clean off.

No exaggeration. He literally slapped her head off her shoulders and it bounced off to parts unknown. Blood fountained up dramatically from her shoulders and then her body collapsed in a heap.

I sprang into action and, following the trail of blood, located her head under a table. Her eyes were still twitching in their sockets. I only had a few seconds…

I picked it up by the hair so she was facing me. "You shouldn't have slapped me!" I yelled at her head. "Violence doesn't solve anything."

Her lips moved ever so slightly. I could see the lights going out so I added, "Who's the retarded one now?"

Everyone was looking at me. Shocked. It was awkward. I'm a horrible person, but usually I can keep it under wraps. I handed her head to an EMT.

> *"Everybody understands a slap in the face."*
> -Jean-Clause Van Damme

the state of distress that results when one perceives a gap between one's desires for social connection and actual experiences of it

You certainly don't need me. Obviously.

And I don't need you, that much is clear. All too clear.

What you need is the idea of me and what I can never lose is the idea of you.

Where would you ever find someone like you when you're with me?

The person I miss the most is me with you.

*** Obviously, the COVID-19 pandemic is a terrible thing and it's the responsibility of every writer to try and contribute something meaningful to readers during this trying time.

Following are some snippets of what appeared on my website during these difficult months. ***

Easter in the time of COVID-19 (the lion tamer)

"So, how's the whip coming?" broadcast Betty across the fence to Barney. They lived next door to each other in a development where each house sat on a quarter acre, so having a conversation as each person sat on their deck was very doable.

Of course, Barney wasn't on his deck at the moment. He was standing in the middle of his backyard practicing the whip. For the life of him, he couldn't get it to crack with any regularity. He replied simply with a small disgruntled grunt. (Hopefully, future writers can just refer to this as a disgrunt.)

"Can I ask about the new dog?" asked Betty. They had been neighbors for years but had never had much of a relationship outside of the occasional friendly nod. Barney's dog sat next to him wearing a large lion's mane wig.

"Sure," replied Barney, once again failing to make the whip crack, which was fortunate for his dog, Lion, because the noise terrified him and would send him sprinting back inside the house. "I'm using this downtime to learn how to be a lion tamer." He said it very matter-of-factly.

"I see," said Betty, "That would explain the platform." She motioned to the large round platform that Barney had built, as if he'd never seen it before. He'd gone to the trouble of stapling a decorative curtain around its base teeming with yellow stars and red stripes and other colorful things.

Another failed attempt at cracking the whip. Lion seemed to breathe a small sigh of relief.

Betty thought that "physical distancing" was a much better way to describe the six feet everyone had been told to keep between each other rather than "social distancing." It seemed much friendlier. It was Easter morning after all.

"You realize that circuses don't do that anymore. The animal rights folks shut it all down." Betty's neighbor on the other side had suddenly cranked up *"Datura"* by Goon to a hundred decibels so she was forced to walk over to the fence to continue the conversation. It was annoying that her neighbor's kids didn't respect the people living around them, but at least the song was good.

Barney stopped whipping and looked at her sincerely. "I know. It's just something I've always wanted to try. To see if I had it in me. That's why I adopted Lion here. Why not use this crisis to better myself, right? Lemons and lemonade and such."

"It's nice you gave a dog a home. So… do you think you could actually get into a cage with a large cat? They seem so ferocious on TV."

Barney looked up into the air as if lost in thought. Finally, his attention returned to Betty and he asked, "Do you want to hear a secret I've never told anyone before?"

If you learn nothing else from my dumb stories, please remember that if anyone ever asks you that question, say "No." Nothing good ever follows. Trust me on that.

Betty smiled and indicated that she did.

"Once, years ago, I was driving and had to pee so I pulled over to a truck stop. After using the urinal, I walked over to wash my hands and saw this long piece of used floss sitting on the sink."

Lion started fidgeting, trying to pull off his mane.

Next-door, *"Datura"* ended and *"Do You Remember the First Time?"* by Pulp started up.

If it seems like I'm stalling, you'll understand why soon enough.

"So, I summoned up all my courage," continued Barney, "and I flossed my teeth with it. Thoroughly. There could have been anything on that floss. It could have been used by anyone. Have you seen trucker's teeth? Maybe a crackhead with gum disease. At that moment, I realized I could do anything. Including, but not limited to, standing in front of a lion."

At that moment, Lion, who thought he was being addressed, jumped up on the platform, which seemed to delight Barney to no end. He said "Good dog!" at least a dozen times and made a big fuss over him.

Betty used the opportunity to slowly walk back inside her house. "Maybe social distancing isn't such a bad way to put it," she said to herself as she closed the sliding glass door behind her.

unexpected heroes of the pandemic

"I hadn't spoken with him in awhile," she told the assembled authorities.

This perplexed them because since the self-quarantine had gone into effect in their township, the two of them had been stuck in the same house. It was a roomy two-story number, but for two people to live in it without talking seemed a bit odd.

Sensing their confusion, she continued. "For the first couple of weeks, everything seemed alright. He actually was using the time to do, as he called them, 'self-improvements.'" She put air quotes around the last two words. There were curious faces pressed against almost every one of her neighbor's windows, watching the little drama unfold. She pretended not to notice.

"I was expecting him to hit the treadmill or learn a second language but instead, he started trying to figure out how to lift only one eyebrow or wiggle his ears." One of the men surrounding her let a small laugh slip. "Then, it progressed to trying to touch his tongue to his elbow. You have to understand, that kind of tomfoolery can get a bit grating." Even she didn't understand why she used the word tomfoolery. She suddenly felt twenty years older and nowhere near as whimsical as she believed herself to be. "He even tried to figure out how to sneeze with his eyes open. Achoo! Achoo! For hours on end. I expected to walk into the kitchen at any time and see his eyeballs sitting on the floor by the refrigerator."

She took a slow breath and unclenched her fists.

"We stopped talking after I walked in our bedroom to find him hopping up and down, doing a weird little dance. He had on a long-sleeve shirt and then another shirt on top of that, but he'd only put his head through. The arms were flopping at his side. He looked at me and said, smiling like an idiot, 'Now I know how an octopus feels.'"

There was a pause that threatened to turn into an uncomfortable pause. Something needed to be said.

"Ma'am, did you consider telling him that an octopus has eight limbs? Clearly, he needed another two arms. Perhaps you could have suggested a light windbreaker," said one of the psychological professionals summoned to the scene.

Behind them, the policemen were loading her husband into the back of a squad car without incident, much to the neighbors' disappointment. There hadn't been a lot to see in the cul-de-sac recently.

"How would that have helped?" the woman asked curtly. Suddenly, the word tomfoolery popped back uninvited into her head.

She rolled on, "I should have seen this coming. All the talk about impossible things, what's possible and what isn't, and then that stupid Amazon delivery…" she trailed off.

Finally someone asked "What stupid delivery?"

She nodded in the direction of her husband. "That stupid black and yellow striped shirt. The costume antenna. The damn bumblebee wings. The whole stupid outfit."

"I see," was all anyone could come up with. "Were you the one who called us?"

"No" she replied. "It was one of those nosy bastards," she said and motioned to her neighbors. "When they saw him on top of the house. I only realized what was happening when I saw the firetruck pull up."

"Must have been quite a shock," said the same psychological professional. "I've seen a lot of strange behavior, but this one is new."

The police car pulled away and it never occurred to the wife to ask where they were taking him.

"We're taking him for observation," came the answer to the unasked question. "It will only be twenty-four hours." Was that disappointment he saw in her eyes?

She could still see his antenna bobbing back and forth in the back of the car as he disappeared into the distance. People started to depart until it was just the two of them.

"Is it true that bumblebees shouldn't be able to fly?" she asked the man. He looked the type that would know that kind of thing.

"That's a myth, ma'am. People used to think their flight defied the laws of physics but scientists figured out that bumblebees just fly differently than other things like planes or birds. We were wrong, not the bumblebees."

The two of them looked at each other. A series of unexpected realizations began to set in. She started to glare at the faces in the windows until one by one, they retreated back into the depths of their homes.

"A windbreaker, huh? That's pretty funny," the woman said. "So... where did you say they're taking my husband? I think I'll follow him over."

"You can follow me. I think I'll head over as well," came his reply.

COVID-19 Update: The First Sunny Day

I'm happy to report that today, we had the first sunny day since the whole coronavirus self-isolation stuff started. Out of nowhere, a perfect day. Blue skies, bright sunshine, and a warm breeze.

So I wanted to take full advantage. Out came the beach towel and the "Ocean Waves on Tropical Island" background sounds on my phone. Once my eyes were closed, I was lying there on a tropical beach.

"Certainly," you might be saying to yourself, "even your daunting powers of imagination cannot overcome the inevitable song of the black-capped chickadee. You must know that the black capped chickadee is not native to tropical climes. 'Poof' goes your tropical beach."

How long have we known each other? You think that type of thing can halt the Manion Express when it gets rolling? I simply assumed that a parrot at some point in its life had spent time near Philadelphia, where it learned to mimic the song of the black-capped chickadee, before returning to its tropical home where it taught that song to its feathered brethren (featheren?).

It was as easy as that.

What wasn't easy was getting comfortable on my towel.

However I lay on my stomach, my neck couldn't find a spot where it didn't hurt.

What I needed was a hole to stick it through, like when I'm on a masseuse table. Not content to let a little thing like that stand in my way, I sprang into action.

"Springing into action" was defined as grabbing my car keys, my wallet, flip flops, a mask, and then heading down to Home Depot. A "mask" was defined as a Lone Ranger mask, because I won't wear a regular one (despite the dirty looks). Where I live, they made it mandatory for people to wear masks when entering any public building, but you'd be surprised how many people will look the other way when someone wearing a Lone Ranger mask strolls into their place of business.

I think they take one look at me and assume it would be too exhausting to explain to me what they meant by "mask."

Moments later, I walked out with a brand new jigsaw.

I don't mean to brag, but I'm quite handy with power tools. It was only about an hour and four splinters later when I'd cut a head-sized hole in my deck. It's my deck, after all. If I want to cut holes in it, why should anyone care?

Throw in a few towels at the edges and the next thing I know, I'm lying flat on my stomach soaking up the sun with my neck as comfy as can be.

Except…

You have no idea how creepy it is underneath a deck. While this was the first day of good weather topside, apparently, under the deck has been Mardi Gras for weeks. All sorts of things were going on in the shadows. Every time I shut my eyes, I heard something rustling or slithering.

It just wasn't acceptable. Completely non-tropical islandish, so I threw on my flip flops and headed back to Home Depot.

Everyone there was just as excited to see me as they were before.

Moments later, I emerged with one of those big industrial lights you see on construction sites.

You can see that Manion is indeed a man of action.

I plugged it in, popped it down the hole, and with one flip of the switch, everything going on under my deck was illuminated.

Truly a mixed blessing.

How many snakes can live under one deck? Every two minutes, I saw another one slithering by. Made it hard to keep my eyes closed and enjoy the sun.

Lest you be mistaken, don't think for a minute that I'm afraid of the dark or garter snakes. What I was a tad nervous about is what eats snakes. There were so many under my deck, it had to be prime hunting ground for creatures that enjoy a little *Thamnophis sirtalis* in their diet. I remember a nature special about a mongoose that made its living eating the biggest snakes it could find, so the last thing I wanted to do was close my eyes and suddenly have a herd of mongeese mauling my face.

"Manion! Get to the part where you talk about cutting a hole in the deck for your balls to go through... so you're not squishing them and whatnot," I hear you saying.

What?! I acknowledge there might have been a time where every other story I wrote included a mention of my balls, but I've grown a lot as a writer since then. Now, I introduce my testicles into a plot only when they are called for (and I no longer refer to them as the Dynamic Duo - real progress).

Plus... if you think I have an aversion to the idea of my face being attacked by mongeese, what makes you think I'd be any more enthusiastic about a frothing mongoose grabbing me by the sack and tugging away while I try to sun myself on my deck?

There. You got the imagery you wanted. Happy?

How did I resolve this issue with the creepy sub-deck? Manion brain-power at its finest.

I put on the Lone Ranger mask when I was on my stomach. No animal is going to mess with the sack of the Lone Ranger. In fact, I'm guessing there were a lot of snakes going back to their nest and saying to the other snakes "You'll never guess who I saw today."

The 2020 COVID-19 Commencement Address

One of the real tragedies of the COVID-19 pandemic was the cancellation of my scheduled commencement address at a prestigious university. I was asked to speak at the graduation ceremonies of The School of Literature, Drama, and Creative Writing at (insert prestigious university here), Class of 2020, and truly feel that these bright-eyed young men and women, hungry for such wisdom, really lost out on the chance to listen to my advice in person. I will provide a transcript here, but honestly, there is no way of capturing the raw magnetism of a Lance Manion presentation.

"Let's start by thinking about writing a story like filling an empty suitcase. An awkward metaphor, I'll admit, but if awkward metaphors make you uncomfortable, you'll end up with nothing but carry-on.

Did you just imagine doing that thing where you put your two hands next to your head and then open them suddenly to indicate that something just blew your mind? I'm guessing you did. I saw a lot of you do it.

Keep listening. There will be even more times when you can put your two hands next to your head and then open them suddenly.

It's my personal belief that *what* you put into the suitcase isn't as interesting as *where* you get the stuff you're putting into it. When you're packing one thing, you're always unpacking another.

Boom. Another one. You're welcome. (Please picture me shooting off a quick wink at the hottest teacher on the stage.)

Where are you getting what you're putting into your story *from*? It's rarely one place. Typically, you're rummaging through the whole house, looking in closets, and opening a dozen drawers. Sometimes looking in places that you don't expect to find anything, but better safe than sorry, am I right?

I'm going to give you a few seconds to catch up. Just the house metaphor should have your head spinning a bit… ironic when you consider that the house I'm talking about *is* your head.

And the 'safe but sorry' throwaway line could be the title of a four-hundred-page book unto itself. A book loaded with charts and graphs, peppered with scholarly quotes and references. A book you don't want to write.

I've actually made my own two hands jump up next to my head and then open suddenly.

Safe but sorry. Safe or sorry. Safe and sorry.

Boom. Boom. Boom.

Did you know that the number-one thing your brain is hardwired to do is to keep you safe? It's a primitive nonconscious part of the brain and it's the reason that 95% of fiction you see on the bookshelves is safe.

It's the reason that most best-selling suitcases don't include anything from the attic or basement. Just shirts. Underwear. Toiletries. The occasional hat.

Nothing to stress you out.

'But Lance, I just want to write a little story about a squirrel that gets injured by a passing car and has to find the courage to drag itself home.'

Bullshit.

Fuck you and fuck your squirrel.

We both know what that squirrel represents. And the car? Why not just call the car what it is.

Your mom.

Courage? Can anyone even define courage these days? Now they call crazy people 'brave.' Am I brave? Are you?

Home? Are you fucking kidding me?

I don't even know where squirrels live. I see them jumping around in trees but I have no idea where they actually sleep. Nests? Burrows? I don't want to know. The more I know about squirrels, the fewer places I can picture them living. I like my squirrels everywhere and nowhere, holding a martini in their paw after a long day of hiding nuts.

There's nowhere like home. Home is where the heart is. Home sweet home.

And you want pack all of this into a squirrel? Why not a fish, Hemingway? Then you could introduce the whole big fish/small pond stuff.

Doesn't SpongeBob have a friend who lives underwater but is also a squirrel? Of course, I believe that she lives in the ocean... small mammal/big ocean doesn't work as well.

There. There it is. Can you feel your brain moving away from safety? The desire to go down into the basement and root around a bit? Only when you have no idea what the next word will be should you ever start to write.

'But Lance, I can actually get *paid* to write a story about a squirrel that gets injured by a passing car and has to find the courage to drag itself home.'

You whore! You disgust me. You and your overbearing parents and fake friends and your New Yorker magazine aspirations.

William S. Burroughs said the following... 'The boy looks into Mugwump eyes blank as obsidian mirrors, pools of black blood, glory holes in a toilet wall closing on the Last Erection.'

So why wouldn't I use this opportunity to shoot a quick wink at that ravishing example of womanhood to my left (the aforementioned hot teacher)? Because I don't need to. That's what language is for.

So, in closing, let me leave you with this. After you're done here and you get your piece of paper saying you can write, giving you permission, you're going to go home. You're going to sit down and figure out what you want to say to this fucked-up world. Travel *will* be involved and drawers and dark corners will have to be explored. Do it boldly. Look everywhere. Make all your squirrels into Mugwumps.

Thank you... and fuck most of you.

Boom."

COVID-19 Update: Not Everyone is a Hero

I went to my local grocery store yesterday and outside was a huge banner that read, "Heroes Work Here."

No, they don't. Just stop it.

Teenagers and people who have made terrible career decisions work there.

One of the many casualties of this coronavirus debacle has been the English language.

> *he·ro* /ˈhirō/ *a person who is admired or idealized for courage, outstanding achievements, or noble qualities.*

Marines and SEALs are heroes. Cops and firemen are heroes. A checkout girl swiping baked beans over a scanner is not.

The same goes with mailmen. They put mail in a mailbox. There is nothing heroic about it. Maybe back in the Pony Express days, riding through dangerous territory with their mailbags full to bursting and bloodthirsty savages lurking around every bluff, maybe then you could call them heroes.

Today? No. Coronavirus or not. An emphatic no.

> *em·phat·ic* /əmˈfadik/ *showing or giving emphasis; expressing something forcibly and clearly.*

Even if they're delivering mail to an Indian reservation. Much different scenario these days. Indians are no longer savage and most haven't even sobered up by the time the mailman has dropped off their mail. The days of cowboys and Indians are long over.

Perhaps the game can be re-invented as Tyrannical Governors and Indians. Because Indians live on reserves of land where they have complete sovereignty, the government can't enforce any COVID regulations on them. If they want to start opening up the casinos, there is squat that the local officials can do about it. This pisses off a lot of people. Which works out for me as I find pissed off people hilarious. Not extraneous to this train of thought: across the globe where the losers of a conflict have been given small areas of land to do with as they like, it has never worked out particularly well for anyone involved. There is something to be said for either forcing the losers to assimilate or just chucking the malcontents into the ocean.

The question I have to ask myself is why I often mention Native Americans when trying to address the coronavirus situation. Is it because I believe that these once-noble peoples would have handled it much better than we did? I just feel like any self-respecting Apache who contracted COVID would just walk off into the woods and die, in consideration for the rest of the tribe. I also feel that Aborigines would share this can-do attitude.

The question you have to be asking yourself is why I referred to Indians as both bloodthirsty savages and once-noble people in the same update. Or, even more relevant, what do either have to do with COVID-19 in the first place?

Perhaps cognitive dissonance is a symptom of COVID-19. Like how bats are terrifying and yet they also keep insect populations under control and pollinate plants. Or how Batman breaks a lot of laws and yet is dedicated to bringing to justice people who prey on others. Not extraneous to this train of thought: it's possible that Batman would feel that the coronavirus was just nature trying to keep human population under control.

One thing is clear… Batman is a hero.

Trash collectors are not. They do a difficult job and are usually under-appreciated, but they are not heroes. It's the same people doing the same job as this time last year. Given the unemployment rates, if they don't want to do it anymore, it would take about ten minutes to find another "hero" to pick up our trash.

Teachers are not heroes. I'm going to say that again; teachers are not heroes. As Norm McDonald once observed, they have the same vacation time as children. And now with online learning... could it get much easier? They can do their job without wearing pants.

Musicians who do concerts in their living room are much appreciated, but not in any way behaving heroically.

I recently read an article that said tattoo artists and dog-walkers are heroes. They most certainly are not.

Which means that some people who write articles are complete dipshits. Stop pandering and have some respect for the language. The word "hero" means something. Don't fuck with that because you want to look like a warmer and more compassionate human being than you really are.

If you say that politicians are heroes, I swear I'm going to rent a Batman costume, hunt you down like the dog you are, and deliver some good old-fashioned justice.

Which, I guess, would make me a hero. Not the hero we need, but the hero we deserve.

COVID-19 Update: Neighbors

Sometimes you forget how long it's been since you had a normal conversation with a stranger. I used to have them all the time.

Now? Nope.

Until yesterday, anyway.

I really should have added "and that's how I like it" after my "nope" to give you some perspective on how I felt when I saw a new neighbor barreling towards me. We were on the same side of the street and a conversation seemed inevitable.

All my fault really. I'd forgotten my mask. If I'd been wearing it as I usually do on my jaunts around the subdivision, I'd have been safe.

Why?

Because I wear a full mask. A children's Halloween mask. Casper the friendly ghost, except I've written the word NO on the forehead. It's my Lance the unfriendly neighbor mask.

But I'd forgotten all about the damn COVID crap as I headed out and the next thing I knew, I was coming to a halt in front of a smiling woman, bracing myself for the awkward few minutes that no doubt lay ahead.

She was well into her third sentence before I realized I should have been listening. Something about a buzzing noise. Something about something hitting her on the head and hurting more than she'd expected.

An odd conversation starter to be sure and I had to scramble to catch up.

"Hmmmmm…. yeah," I started off. So far, so good.

"I'm not sure how far it had fallen," she said.

Because I didn't have the heart to tell her I wasn't listening to her story when she disclosed exactly what it was that fell on her head, I was a bit flummoxed.

"Yeah, that gravity… yep," I offered as a reply.

She increased the diameter of her smile until I could see teeth that had not previously been on display.

Feeling I should contribute something, I said, "It's that damn terminal velocity. If it had been falling long enough, it hit your head at 122 miles per hour."

"Really?" she asked, her head tilting slightly like my dog does when I interrupt her licking herself.

"No wonder it hurt!" she finally added. "Anything hitting your head at that speed would leave a mark."

Finally, she said something that piqued my curiosity. It was the way she said "Anything." Such certainty. Such pomposity.

"A roll of toilet paper?" I inquired.

The teeth that until recently had been tucked away behind her lips returned to a tucked state.

"Even if it fell from space," I half-asked, half-stated, trying to figure it out in my head. "If it fell from too high up, it would burn up in reentry. I imagine whatever fat kid happened to be looking through his telescope would really be puzzled by that. Make a wish, fatty."

I laughed. She didn't.

Don't ask me why it had to be a fat kid. I hoped she didn't have a fat kid at home waiting for her. Maybe it was my subconscious missing my Halloween mask, but I immediately thought of a sky filled with flaming rolls of toilet paper raining down. The ultimate cosmic TPing.

She tried to change to topic.

"So, how are you doing through all this self-isolation?" she asked.

Maybe it was all the talk about toilet paper, but I immediately thought I'd open up and share.

"They should have warned everybody that the toilet paper shortage was only going to be temporary," I said with exaggerated anger.

She looked at me, waiting for me to finish the thought. I thought the thought was finished but if she really needed me to finish, I didn't want to disappoint.

"The thing is, when it first started, there was that big run on toilet paper. Everybody said there were going to be shortages and we'd all end up using newspaper and leaves, so I went out and bought as much as I could get my hands on."

At this point, I could barely see her front two teeth.

"The worst part was that I bought anything I could, including that budget toilet paper. Some of it's so thin, you need to use a whole handful." I held my fist aloft to illustrate just how much I was talking about.

"Ironic that the quality is shitty when you consider what it's used for. And then there's the stuff that you can use to sand your deck with. Rough business."

I looked up at the clear sky, to indicate what a delightful evening I thought it was. As if on cue, a light breeze whipped through my hair. I have to admit, I momentarily felt a bit charming.

"Now, I have three rolls of toilet paper by the toilet and every session, I have to decide if I'm up to using a bargain brand. Like life isn't complicated enough…"

She nodded her agreement. Sort of. Agreement… bewilderment… they look so similar.

"Usually, I use the good stuff in the morning. Start the day off right. It's the afternoons that I typically feel my anus is up to the challenge and I'll mix in a bit of the coarser variety."

It was right then that I realized I was enjoying talking to someone else. After all the trepidation, it turns out I actually miss dialogue with other living, breathing people.

She excused herself and began her walk home. I was sad to see her go. "Watch out for that falling TP!" I yelled cheerfully after her.

I wonder what hit her head. Probably a dragonfly.

COVID-19 Update: Getting Hosed

How boring is it getting in Casa de Manion?

Here's how boring it's getting: Today, I actually poured myself a glass of water to take into the bathroom as I peed. I wanted to feel water entering my body as it exited. The Circle of Urine and whatnot.

That's the kind of thing you do when all other forms of entertainment have evaporated.

I guess when I think about it, it would really need to be raining into my open mouth to really close the loop.

Problem was, rain or no, just as I started drinking, the water went down the wrong pipe. I'm not sure if this is what happens when you pee or if it was just a coincidence, but I had no time to debate such things because once I started coughing, the peeing became a bit tricky.

For my devoted female readers, I can only ask you to imagine holding a hose between your legs where a man's penis resides and then try to aim water into a bucket as you cough violently.

How boring is it getting in Casa de Manion?

Here's how boring it's getting: As soon as I suggested that any female reading this should go outside and pretend a hose is their penis, I had to find out if the experience is actually equivalent.

That's right. I marched right out into my yard, stuck a hose between my legs, and pretended it was nestled up against my vagina. Right in full view of neighbors and passing cars alike.

You could argue that nobody knew what I was actually doing, but let me tell you, they knew something horrible was transpiring right in front of their eyes. Maybe it was the way I was gripping the hose or maybe it was all the coughing and flailing, but they knew. Oh, they knew alright. I didn't care though. A neighbor locked eyes with me, imploring me to make it known what it was I was up to, but I just hissed, "Your witchcraft won't work here."

Maybe it was how feminine I felt for a brief moment. Pretending to be a girl pretending to be a guy brought up some really odd emotions. Complicated stuff. I'm not even going to tell you what else I thought about doing with the hose. Let's just say I would probably be incarcerated had I followed through with some of the notions. I originally typed urges but given my new feminine status, I'm not sure that would have been accurate.

How bored is it getting in Casa de Manion?

Well, it's so bored, I won't even bother to acknowledge that "How bored is it getting in Casa de Manion?" is grammatically wrong. I'm so bored, I don't even want to use the language correctly. Fuck yo' words. Instead, I'm going to wonder if you bothered to read Casa de Manion with the right accent or just galloped past an opportunity to be whimsical. Did you read it Man-yun or, correctly for this particular ethnic application, Man-yon?

If saying it didn't bring a smile to your face, then you're not saying it correctly. Put in some effort or you're just wasting your time.

In his book *Model of Human Occupation,* Gary Kielhorner writes;

"All that humans do exists in the framework of time. Time reveals itself as a vacuum, inviting us to fill it with doing. Without action, time weighs heavily upon us.
Consequently, we are moved to fill or occupy time with the things we do. Doing unfolds in the stream of time, carrying us forth, marking time's passing, and shaping the nature of things in the next moment. Consequently, our doing fills the present and anticipates the temporal horizon just beyond us."

And to think this started off about a stream. A warm yellow stream that took some unexpected twists and turns and splashes and drips and in the process, killed some time. That led to an unexpected thought that took me into my yard and killed more time. It took patience not to tell my neighbors to fuck off, killing even more time… and any chance I might have had to be invited to the upcoming block party.

And feeling feminine for those glistening, complicated moments made me glad I took my phone out of my pants before going outside and playing with the hose. Had I not, I might have taken a very complicated chance and asked someone to spend some of our fleeting time together.

"Time is a great teacher, but unfortunately it kills all its pupils."

-Hector Berlioz

COVID-19 Update: the Realtor

She knew she was violating about a dozen oaths she'd sworn as a realtor, to protect her client's privacy and such, but the picture that greeted her on the wall in the hall of the cute split-level had really set off an emotional wild goose chase and once she had the scent of goose… ethics be damned.

She was the type of girl, and realtor, who made it impossible to describe her actions without run-on sentences.

The picture on the wall was, presumably, of the owner of the dwelling as a much-younger man. Although "man" might be a stretch. In fairness to this author, who already has to deal with a character with run-on sentences, describing him as a much-younger young man would be a crippling blow to my literary integrity.

Not quite a man but more than a boy and packing one hell of a mullet.

Just like someone she knew in college.

In fact, under the mullet lurked a face that could have easily been mistaken for his. It was eerie how similar they were.

Why would this set off a goose-chase?

I'll let you come to your own conclusions.

Not thirty seconds later, she walked into his study and saw the very same artwork hanging over his desk that hung in the bedroom of the individual she used to know. And because there were guitars littering the room.

She hesitated to go through his closets… but she did.

She didn't think it was appropriate to go through his drawers... but she did that as well.

And then, with trembling hands, she leaned forward to see what he was on his iPod. If he was going to leave it lying around, then he should expect strangers rummaging through his house to rummage through his subconscious.

She listened with the intensity of the accused watching a jury coming back into the courtroom to announce their verdict.

Guilty! Not only was it a song that would be playing in whatever romantic movie she could see herself starring in, the name of the damn song was *"Just Like a Movie" (Wallows).* She saw herself moving towards him in slow motion as the music started... no. No she didn't! She shook her head until the scenes departed.

Not just like a movie.

Whoever this guy was, he was a doppelganger. There was no other conclusion to draw.

At this point, you might be asking yourself a big fat "So what? What's wrong with a little goose-chasing in the middle of an otherwise-dull day?"

It's at this next point that regular readers of my website, you know who you are, are just breathing a sigh of relief that I didn't wedge in a made up a word like dopplegooser or gooserganger. That will teach you a little lesson about premature sighs of relief.

By the end of this story, you might also learn a thing or two about sighs in general.

When the realtor was done sighing and looking off into the distance, although the distance in this case was time rather than the physical space she found herself occupying (in retrospect I should have said "looking back into the distance"), she realized she needed to know if he was married.

Not that she was anticipating making a play for this mysterious stranger, although most of the romantic movies she sees herself starring in start with this premise, she was just curious if his wife was her doppelganger.

> *dop·pel·gäng·er / 'däpəl̩ˌgaNGər/ noun an apparition or double of a living person*

You're welcome.

> *dopplegooser / 'däpəl̩ˌgOOSər/ noun   see gooserganger*

My apologies.

Anyway… the photo album was under his bed. She sat down and flipped through it. The man had indeed married a woman just like her. She watched the much-younger young man grow into a full-blown man and realized it had been a long time since she last cried. She didn't even care that some of the tears splashed onto the fading pictures.

Was that longing she felt? Regret?

She considered hanging around until the man arrived home. To see him in the flesh. This dopplegooserganger.

She considered calling the man that he reminded her of. To hear his voice.

She considered staging a break-in and stealing the picture that hung over the stranger's desk.

Instead, she sighed and slid the photo album back under the bed. After allowing her heart to ache a little longer, she walked out, put the front door key back under the mat, and drove home.

Just like she knew she would.

Why was she so upset?

You know why.

We all know why.

What did I tell you about sighs?

In the movies she sees herself starring in, they would all have that little extra bit after all the credits have rolled like the superhero movies do.

It would show her walking towards her car saying, "Don't ask yourself questions that you don't want an honest answer to. The water is not holding back the dam."

It would show her driving home. Windows down and wind whipping through her hair. Finding a good song to listen to.

The song would start playing and the camera would slowly pull away until her car became just another vehicle on the crowded freeway.

The song would be *"Closure Blues"* (Jim Arkus).

We would hear her voice singing along.

> *"It's not like the verses put down on a*
> *page, 'cause the poets...they are wrong.*
> *So it's a shame for me to say,*
> *but it's time for me to be moving on."*

Sigh.

Fade to black.

COVID 19 Update: Mold

Everyone knows the story of how penicillin was discovered. For those of you who aren't everyone, don't get down on yourself; more people aren't everyone than you'd think. Let me recap. Back in 1928, Sir Alexander Fleming, returning from a family vacation, saw that a sample of staphylococcus bacteria he had left lying around had been killed when some of the mold he had invented fell into the dish. Thus was born the world's first antibiotic and, through the hard work and dedication of numerous other scientists throughout the following decades, millions of lives were saved.

But at what cost?

I have yet to find out what Mr. Fleming was up to inventing *penicillium notatum* in the first place. Like there wasn't enough mold knocking about the planet as is.

Let's be clear, mold is bad stuff. Some mold causes allergic reactions and respiratory problems while other molds also produce mycotoxins that can pose serious health risks, including neurological problems and in some cases, death.

And on top of all that? It makes things slimy. If you go to make yourself a sandwich and the meat is all shiny and slippery, I can guarantee you that dollars to donuts, mold is involved.

And we want to celebrate a man who invented another mold?! I don't have any facts to support me on this, but I'll wager that last week when I had to toss out that roast beef sandwich, which took me no less than ten minutes to make, that Sir Alexander's mold was probably the culprit. The damn thing was bristling with spores.

A few million lives saved and we're all supposed to just gloss over this?

As I said before, nobody has ever asked him why he was fooling around with molds in the first place. Clearly, the fact that it ended up killing bacteria was just a crazy coincidence. If that's the case, what did he originally plan to do with this new mold, outside of fucking up my sandwiches 92 years in the future?

And where the hell was he vacationing? I'm the only one who finds that suspicious? One minute, he's ass-deep in mold research and then suddenly, he's conveniently off jet-skiing in the Caribbean?

Yes, jet-skiing- in 1928. It's common knowledge that scientists have all the cool shit way before we get hold of it.

It's all very fishy.

All I'm saying is you have to keep a close eye on scientists - especially ones that decide to work with molds. Molds, fungi, bacteria. Anything you can't see with the human eye. We're basically just taking their word for most of what they're doing. Crashing around, wearing white coats, and filling up beakers and test tubes all day. And if you ask them what they're doing, they just look at you and say, "You wouldn't understand. Now if you'll excuse me, I have to take a vacation."

I'm guessing this damn COVID virus was created under similar shady circumstances.

I bet the guy who invented it is named Arex Freming.

COVID-19 Update: Online Shopping

As if COVID wasn't bad enough, now you can't even go to the mall without running into feral packs of domestic terrorists beating the shit out of white people and interrupting meals at the food court with requests to raise a Black Power fist.

Where does that leave people like me who are uncomfortable with the online shopping experience?

I'll tell you. Fucked.

I've never been able to navigate the choppy waters of retail websites. I'll spend twenty minutes thinking I'm buying something only to find myself back at the homepage where I started. The only thing having been accomplished is giving my credit card information to another store that's only hours from getting hacked. But recently, knowing my mall options were no longer on the table, and knowing that a change of season was right around the corner, and with it, the appropriate garments needed to be worn, I sat down and attempted to buy some clothes online.

Fast forward to a series of packages being delivered to my home over the next few days. Obviously, if everything went well, I wouldn't be writing this.

Let me ask you a question. Have you ever heard of people selling used clothes online?

Of course you haven't! What kind of demented mind thinks to sell old clothes online?! There should have been a giant red warning label on the link that brought me to these clothes saying "Danger! Used clothes being sold here!"

I had no idea. It never even occurred to me that someone would be peddling used clothes. I just thought I found some sellers offering exceptional values.

When I unwrapped my first parcel, I couldn't wait to put the shirt on and admire myself in the mirror. Having done so, two things became very clear to me: 1) it had a mustard stain on the front of it, and 2) the person who last wore this shirt was no longer alive.

It reeked of nursing home. The smell was overwhelming. There was no mistaking it.

My head swam.

"No wonder it was only five dollars. You fool."

I felt violated. Somebody was obviously clearing out the closets of the dead and selling their clothes to unsuspecting suckers like myself. Sure enough, over the next few days, I assembled a wardrobe that would have looked completely appropriate at any old folk's home in the country.

Here's a bit of trivia. You can't wash out the smell of nursing home. You can wash something ten times with the most powerful flowery scents known to mankind and it will come out of the dryer ready to be put onto the comatose body of a ninety-year-old. When wearing that shirt, whatever drink you pour yourself will end up prune juice. The music of Lawrence Welk will play uninvited in your head.

I have to admit it made me examine my fashion sense a bit. Why was I attracted to the clothing of a bygone era in the first place?

By the end of the week, the delivery guy would walk up my driveway holding the package at arm's length, his face letting it be known that he not only didn't want to smell like nursing home the rest of the day, but he didn't appreciate me desecrating the closets of the recently deceased.

"I'm not the tomb-robber here!" I felt like yelling after him, "I'm the victim. I didn't know…" But I didn't bother. Who would believe a man who smelled like I did? If dementia ever made a cologne…

I'm wearing one of the shirts now. What else can I do? It seems not only wasteful to throw them away, but somehow disrespectful. Someone somewhere used to wear this shirt. Shuffling around the retirement community, trying his best to look dapper. Not cool. Dapper. It's much harder to attain dapper-status.

So here I sit, neither dapper nor cool, smelling like the soon-to-be departed. Trying to wear the shirt to the best of my ability as a tribute to someone I never met. Trying to live up to the expectations of someone I invented in my head.

Damn Black Lives Matter. Damn them to hell.

*** Enough COVID already. Let's end with some Nap Lapkin, shall we? ***

Rudolph the Brown-Nosed Reindeer (as told by Nap Lapkin)

There is simply nowhere more depressing to be than at a bar approaching closing time on Xmas Eve.

By eleven o'clock, after all the revelers have departed, the only people left are those with nowhere to go and no one to go home to.

Which is why Nap Lapkin, super-agent extraordinaire, was perched on a stool eyeballing a beautiful woman sitting alone. His on-again, off-again girlfriend Madonna was spending the holidays with her family (Nap wasn't quite ready to be introduced into that heartwarming scenario), so he was hoping that perhaps with a dose of the ol' Lapkin charm, Santa wouldn't be the only one coming tonight. Put another way, it was not her stocking he wanted to stuff.

(A bit crude for a Xmas story, I'll admit, but when you're reporting on Nap Lapkin, you have to maintain your journalistic integrity and tell it like it is.)

Noting what she was drinking, Nap procured another and headed over to her table bearing gifts.

"Have you ever heard the story of Rudolph the Brown-Nosed Reindeer?" he asked as he sat down next to her.

Startled, she could only look at him.

Noting the name on the employee ID badge that hung off her t-shirt, he punctuated his inquiry with "Erica." He also noted she had obviously been working the day before Xmas and a psychological profile began to take shape. (You'll note that being a super-agent involves a lot of noting things.)

"May I?" he inquired and, because he'd already sat down and she was unsure of exactly what Nap was asking, she thought it over carefully and decided to remain startled.

"You see, Rudolph came up with that other Rudolph. The one with the red nose. Like Rudolph with the red nose, this Rudolph wasn't a particularly strong flyer. But what he was good at was kissing up. Every time Santa would stop by to watch their progress, he would go into full ass-kissing mode. Eventually, he earned the nickname Rudolph the Brown-Nosed Reindeer."

Erica picked up the drink Nap had brought over and went from a startled state to one that can be best described as a less-startled one.

"Once it was clear to the reindeer responsible for selecting the team to pull Santa's sleigh that our boy wasn't going to make the cut, they reassigned Rudolph to Admin."

Nap noted that Erica's posture changed when she heard that. Her ID badge was standard Government Issue. Obviously he had hit a nerve, so he went with it.

"You see, what they don't tell you is that there's a lot more to delivering gifts to every child on the planet than eight reindeer pulling a sleigh," Nap continued.

"I bet," Erica said, nodding her appreciation for those involved in logistics.

"Santa has to find somewhere to land to deliver all the gifts and there are a lot of areas where that's a real challenge. Have you ever seen the movie *Apollo 13*?"

Erica replied that it was one of her favorites.

Nap noted that as well.

"Well, Rudolph was like the Gary Sinise character. Except in this case, Rudolph was in and out of the sleigh simulator dozens of times every Xmas Eve. Working out tricky landings and such."

"Wow," was all his buxom companion could come up with.

A lesser man would have pivoted and started to ask the woman personal questions in a clumsy effort to move the relationship along, but not Nap Lapkin.

Lapkin was a pro. He knew when he was playing a winning hand. He noted the living shit out of it.

He continued with the story.

"The thing that people who live in buildings with state-of-the-art security forget is that the right jolly ol' elf needs access to their tree. Without Rudolph, Santa is sitting outside, bag in hand. Someone has to hack into the system to allow entry."

Erica smiled broadly. It was obvious her job was somehow connected to IT.

Nap sensed it was time for closing arguments. "One foggy night, and Mr. Red-Nose is a household name but slave away behind the scenes for years and you can't get the time of day, let alone a TV special!"

Of all the noting that took place that evening, Nap failed to note he was far more red-nosed than brown in his personal affairs (self-awareness rarely makes it onto holiday wish lists). In fact, a number of health professionals employed by a variety of agencies who'd come into contact with Nap over the years would testify that he was completely and entirely 100% Grade A certified red-nosed. Erica remained blissfully unaware of this fact.

Returning to the action, we find Nap reaching a glorious, alcohol-fueled crescendo…

"Have you ever tried to hack into a mainframe with hooves? Have you?! Obviously not because we have hands!" Nap bellowed, clearly carried away with his story. Everyone in the bar momentarily swung their attention his way. He showed them that he did indeed have hands.

After a moment, he collected himself.

"Why did you tell me that story?" asked a transfixed Erica.

After mulling it over a bit, Nap replied "Because my creator put me here in this bar tonight to tell it to you. I am simply a vessel."

(Talk about a serious next-level "fourth wall" moment. Is he referring to me or God? I hope you take a moment to fully absorb and double-fully appreciate his reply.)

"Would you like to come back to my place?" inquired his prey, completely oblivious to the "fourth wall" implications.

Well, at the Whoville Tavern, they say – that Nap's large penis grew three sizes that day.

Nap Lapkin turns down a mission

"So, let me get this straight," said Nap Lapkin, trying to get things straight. "You want me to track down a tall, middle-aged man with brown hair that you both met when you were in your early teens?"

Both Billy Joel and James Taylor, sitting across from him in his living room, nodded their agreement. Eagerly at that.

Perhaps some catching up is in order.

Years ago, after some awards show or other, Billy and James got to talking. Talking and drinking. After many hours of discussing the ups and downs of celebrity, Billy happened to mention an incident that took place shortly after his first piano lesson. Made quite an impression on him. He couldn't have been much more than twelve. Real sixth-drink type of sharing.

"I don't expect you to believe me, but I swear to god its true…" and then he went on to describe the encounter. Not the entire encounter because after a few sentences, James' jaw fell open and he finished the story for him.

"I had the same damn thing happen only hours after picking up a guitar for the first time. I never told anyone because I didn't think they'd believe me."

Nap stood up and, after pouring himself another drink (an Irish Car Bomb - 3/4 pint Guinness Stout, 1/2 shot Bailey's Irish Cream, 1/2 shot Jameson Irish Whiskey... in case you ever want to drink like a spy), sat back down. Where else are you going to get this kind of action?

"Even if I was to bring in a sketch artist and have you two describe him down to a mole on his neck, that was decades ago. He'd look nothing like you remember him." Nap remained seated, content that he'd made an air-tight case against continuing the conversation.

The real problem Nap was having was that he was enjoying having two of the biggest musical icons on the planet in his home asking him for his help. It was embarrassing.

You know why people pay boatloads of money for floor seats at a basketball game or front row seats to a concert when there are obviously better places to be if you want a good view? The reason is that they hope to overhear an interaction between people who are famous. It's that simple. They want a little glimpse into that world.

Nap wanted to be above such things, but when he opened his front door and saw the two of them standing outside, he felt a rush of whatever it is that makes people act like idiots in front of other people. "Billy Joel poops. He poops. He farts and then poop comes out of his very normal and average Piano Man rectum," he found himself muttering under his breath as they walked into the house.

He was embarrassed... and an embarrassed Nap is a dangerous Nap.

"But Nap," James Taylor said/pled, "we were told you were the best at this kind of stuff. It's not just the two of us either. Same thing happened to Pete Townshend and Willie Nelson."

"Willie Nelson, huh?" snorted Nap, clearly showing that he did not put much stock in any recollection had by someone who'd spent his entire life high as a kite. "Although '*Always on My Mind*' is a pretty amazing song."

"Ok, forget Willie," piped up Billy, "But this might be some time-traveling mystery man. Certainly, you have to be curious." My apologies for including both a Willie and a Billy in the same sentence. Way too much illy. You wouldn't catch Steinbeck doing that sort of thing.

"Curious? Curious about what?" said a clearly annoyed Nap.

"The same guy, years apart, visits famous musicians long before they are famous to discuss their lives, influences and motivations and you don't find that odd? How did he know who would become famous?" inquired a clearly annoyed Billy.

James, annoyed but more adept at hiding it, piled on, "He actually told me he'd have no interest in talking to me once I'd achieved notoriety. He said that success ruins everything and the only conversations that matter are the ones that take place beforehand. How could he possibly know I'd go on to become a big, famous musician? I'd just literally picked up a guitar."

"Clearly fellas, I don't consider this a matter of national security," replied a still-embarrassed Nap.

Clearly, it had been awhile since either Billy Joel or James Taylor had been called fella.

"I have to be honest, I haven't liked any of your songs since '*Allentown,*' Bill. And James... what has it been...about a hundred and thirty years since '*Fire and Rain?*' Maybe that guy was on to something."

The recently-dubbed fellas turned on their heels and stormed out of Nap's abode.

I wrestled with whether I should call them "recently-dubbed" or "freshly-minted" fellas. I just thought you should know. Some people believe that I just plop down any damn words that come into my head, but I feel it's important to set the record straight from time to time. I lovingly craft each and every sentence.

Well... some of them.

Like the sentence "James, annoyed but more adept at hiding it, piled on" that appeared earlier in the story. The two proceeding sentences had described the speakers as clearly annoyed. I had planned on saying "James, clearly annoyed but more adept at hiding it, piled on," which would have cemented the fact that I am at the height of my literary powers (flashing a casual yet dazzling burst of meter and rhythm), but I couldn't bring myself to do it because I couldn't reconcile how something could be clearly hidden. I know it would have come off as awkward and I just couldn't do that to you.

The point being, you've read about all the crazy missions Nap has been on and I thought it was time you read about one that he turned down. A shame really, I could have made something wonderful out of this strange figure who had visited Billy and James. Probably 300 pages or more of wonderful. Maybe even a feature-length film. But I couldn't do that to Nap.

He'd spend the whole adventure being embarrassed.

So fuck Billy Joel and James Taylor (flashing a casual yet dazzling burst of profanity).

About the Author

What can you say about Lance Manion that hasn't been said before? Almost everything.

not every story is about you…

but you're in all of them